MORE DRIFTING
THAN ROWING -

A Journey Down The River Wye

By

Richard Blackshaw

Copyright © Richard Blackshaw 2019
This book is sold subject to the condition that it shall not, by way of trade or otherwise, be lent, resold, hired out, or otherwise circulated without the publisher's prior consent in any form of binding or cover other than that in which it is published and without a similar condition including this condition being imposed on the subsequent publisher.
The moral right of Richard Blackshaw has been asserted.
www.theriverwye.co.uk
ISBN-13: 9781075461200

This book has not been created to be specific to any individual's or organizations' situation or needs. Every effort has been made to make this book as accurate as possible. This book should serve only as a general guide and not as the ultimate source of subject information. This book contains information that might be dated and is intended only to educate and entertain. The author shall have no liability or responsibility to any person or entity regarding any loss or damage incurred, or alleged to have incurred, directly or indirectly, by the information contained in this book.

DEDICATION

*To the doctors, nurses and staff of Salford Royal and Christie Hospitals,
to whom I shall be ever grateful.*

Review

"Amusing, informative and inspirational, reminds of my younger days canoeing the Wye."
- Rex Tasker
Oscar-nominated documentary filmmaker

CONTENTS

Acknowledgements i
Preface 1
Preamble Ramble! 2
Introduction 13
CHAPTER 1 *Just a thought!* 17
CHAPTER 2 *Make Ready* 29
CHAPTER 3 *Off we go!* 36
CHAPTER 4 *To boldly go!* 43
CHAPTER 5 *What Rapids?* 52
CHAPTER 6 *Boats Small and Big* 65
CHAPTER 7 *Four-Star Camping and Beyond* 75
CHAPTER 8 *Italian Romanesque and Aussies* 87
CHAPTER 9 *Oh, what a beautiful morning!* 103
CHAPTER 10 *Sad Farewell to Ducks!* 118
CHAPTER 11 *Stones Again!* 135
CHAPTER 12 *Romantic Tourism & Not!* 148
CHAPTER 13 *Mud, Mud, Glorious Mud!* 165
River Wye Adventure Recipes 176
Reference Sources 183
Quotes 185
About the Author 188

Acknowledgements

Special thanks to:

My sons Adam and James for their continued encouragement and support.

Alan for logistical support.

Mac for his help at Chepstow.

The management and staff of the Lucksall Campsite.

Front cover photograph by the kind permission of Dominic Gribbin.

Preface

"Believe me, my young friend; there is nothing – absolutely nothing – half so much worth doing as simply messing about in boats."

Ratty, The Wind in the Willows.

The problem with rowing, is that it's done backwards. Therefore, you can't see where you're going, only where you've been!

I did intend to be diligent in checking the course ahead or should I say behind, but the splendour of the River Wye valley provided many distractions. My gaze would be taken and held by spectacular limestone cliffs and gorges, views of magnificent wooded escarpments or the close proximity of water fowl with their young, undisturbed by my quiet passage.

The alarming consequence of my inattention to navigation, was a surprising 'thwack' on the back of the head from the branch of an overhanging tree, or coming to a dead stop due to running aground or hitting some half-submerged boulder, which did on more than one occasion, send me sprawling over backwards!

I'd hoped for a river adventure in stunning countryside and that was what my 104-mile journey through an 'Area of Outstanding Natural Beauty' provided. To explore the River Wye by boat was an experience I will never forget and would recommend to all. My decision to camp along the way was justified and indeed, added to the whole escapade. Memories of all the humorous incidents and encounters, far too numerous to relate in this minor tome, will stay with me forever, as would those of all the helpful, generous and fascinating people I met along the way.

Preamble Ramble!

"Absorbed in the new life he was entering upon, intoxicated with the sparkle, the ripple, the scents and the sounds and the sunlight, he trailed a paw in the water."

Mole, The Wind in the Willows.

I

Like all children I was fascinated by water. Nearby streams, canals and reservoirs provided endless fun and numerous near fatal experiences. One of our favourite activities was the regular damming of the local woodland streams. My pals and I would toil happily for hours, constructing robust dams from large stones and sod. We would make quick visits home for food and upon returning take satisfaction from our efforts, having flooded a sizeable area of woodland.

Once the word of our endeavours went around, more willing labourers and budding hydro-engineers arrived from far and wide to assist with construction and necessary constant 'plugging up' of the dam, to foil the now considerable water's attempts to break free. The workforce was divided into two groups; the younger and less experienced boys were charged with foraging for suitable dam material, like a large stone or good piece of earthy sod, which was supplied to a member of the elder and more experienced team, to be placed and positioned with great care and precision into the great dam.

Eventually, escaping water would become too great to plug, causing us to hurriedly abandon our handiwork for the safety of higher ground. Although disappointed to see our good work slowly disintegrate under the considerable water pressure, we enjoyed watching the surging tumult break free and sweep all before it. These were the carefree days. We would learn much later that local outbreaks of polio were attributed to playing in dirty water, but on the positive side, leptospirosis had not yet been invented.

I suppose it was a natural development that we should introduce rafting to our adventures. I can't remember whose idea it was, but on one occasion we had created our own Amazon basin and achieved an impressive depth of water, when it was suggested that we should build a raft and ply back and forth across our new inland sea, like Thor Heyerdahl crossing the Pacific Ocean on his balsa raft 'Kon-Tiki'. We again split into two work parties. One group went off to borrow planks from a nearby abandoned wooden fence, the other returned to their homes to requisition saws, hammers and large nails.

We relied upon the older boys for their knowledge of marine design, but sadly our raft would not support more than two of us at a time. This meant that I had to wait ages for my turn on the craft to come around again, but it was great fun poling along. Needless to say, nearly all of us overbalanced and fell in at some time, ending up soaked to the skin. We would race home as quickly as we could for a change of dry clothes, but more importantly so not to miss our next turn on the raft. Of course as with all good things, parents got to hear of our exploits and put an end to it.

When in our penultimate year at junior school, four weeks before our long awaited five-week summer holiday, we enjoyed a two-week local holiday towards the end of June. As we approached this time, teaching became more relaxed. So for the last half an hour of every day our teacher would read aloud from some suitable children's classic.

The chosen book was Kenneth Graham's *The Wind in the Willows*. No doubt the intended purpose was to use Toad's lack of moral fortitude as a life lesson, but all that was lost on me. I was totally captivated by Ratty's enthusiasm for the river and boats and Mole's enjoyment of experiencing boating for the first time.

We celebrated the first day of our holiday by playing endless cricket on the village green. Living close to a railway line, our lives were punctuated by the times of passing steam trains. We would race out of school in time, to spot the name and number of the 4.15pm Patriot class engine, pulling a goods train to Carlisle. Equally, all evening football and cricket games were suspended as we sped to watch the seven o'clock Jubilee class from Manchester thunder by.

On this particular warm summer's evening, we decided to watch the passing trains from the buttress of a much explored culvert enabling a stream to pass under the rail track. The trains came and went and as we moved off homewards, we noted that recent civil engineering had created a steep-sided valley for this stream after it passed through a newly constructed road culvert. It was now ideally suited for some serious damming, so plans were made for the next day.

Early next morning, wearing our 'wellies' we started converting the shallow stream into a miniature Hoover Dam. Conveniently, the bank of the stream was littered with large stone blocks from some long-gone building. Although heavy, these oblong blocks were ideal and as we added another course along the dam, the water level increased by over six inches. Another pal became aware that the stream passing his house had suddenly become considerably higher, so suspecting some damming was in progress, came to investigate.

We had created more of a weir than a dam, but felt very satisfied that we had raised the water level to about four feet, creating a new canal roughly eight feet wide and extending several hundred yards. Our newly arrived pal had a magnificent idea. Behind his garden shed was an old tin bath which he suggested would make an ideal boat. In earlier times, this mighty tin bath would have been brought in and placed before the kitchen fire and filled with kettles of hot water for family bathing, but had long been redundant due to the advent of indoor plumbing. No sooner said than done, the three of us managed to remove the bath from the back garden without being observed and carried it to its launching site.

Excitedly, we slid the bath into the water and there it valiantly rode the waves like the Queen Mary. Tentatively, my braver pal climbed in and to our surprise, the bath was both very buoyant and being flat bottomed very stable. The tin bath was great for two, but with three the water came frighteningly near to its top edge. The bath owner had to leave as he and family were going away on holiday for two weeks, but told us to make sure we put the bath back before his family returned home.

The two us had a marvellous time. Using long sticks we would punt the bath as far as we could up stream, then sitting either end, would slowly drift back downstream to our newly constructed weir. We never tired of this game, all day every day for about four days. As we added more courses of blocks and support to our dam, our navigation became longer, allowing us to explore further into previously unchartered territories of suburban back gardens. We became commandos on a deadly mission; keeping low in our landing craft, we silently glided past the enemy as they gardened or hung out washing. Periodically we would moor our craft and by stealth, make our way behind enemy lines to source vital supplies of chocolate and pop.

Even aged ten, my pal and I gained pleasure from slowly drifting with the slight current, bathed in dappled sunlight as we passed under hawthorns and sycamores. Passage through the new under-road culvert became difficult, as the ever-increasing water level lifted us nearer the roof. Oh what fun we had. Unknown to us at the time, the increased water level some considerable distance upstream had caused concern, so the local authority sent workmen to investigate. We were just about to remove our bath from its camouflaged hiding place on the morning in question, when we saw the council men surveying our impressive stone-built weir. Needless to say, they demolished our great construction and ruined our pleasure. But we really had a happy few days.

II

I subscribe to the notion that our parents must bear the responsibility for our negative actions as well as our positive ones. My father also enjoyed anything to do with boats. They were strategic to his enjoyment of our annual holidays taken in the Lake District and Cornwall. Equally should any destination have a lake, offering boats to row or motor, my father would take advantage of the facility, with me in tow.

However, as a child these marine outings were pure purgatory as my father always had to be captain and therefore, always steered, helmed or rowed. As I was fascinated with boats, having to just sit there, not being allowed to take the wheel, tiller or oar was torture. On boating lakes and such, I would see other kids beaming from ear to ear as they rowed or handled the tiller under the watchful eye of proud fathers. But not mine, as he always had to be in control.

Presumably there was some deep-rooted psychological reason for my father's behaviour? But as he did with boats in my younger days, he would do the same with cars later in my teenage years, which provoked my similar response.

So it was only natural when aged eleven I should take matters into my own hands. We routinely spent our Easter holiday at hotels along the shores of Lake Derwent Water, near Keswick in the Lake District. This particular hotel provided two rowing boats for use by patrons. One was a twelve-foot plywood dinghy, the other being a typical sixteen foot or so clinker-built, Edwardian-style lake rowing boat, the type that can still be hired on most lakes today.

Plans for us to take the twelve-foot dinghy out trout fishing that day had been cancelled, so I was left to my own devices. I decided to wander down to the lakeside where the hotel's boats were kept. The larger boat was beached, but the ply dinghy was invitingly bobbing about on the lake, gently straining at its painter tied to the small wooden jetty. Having passed a time skimming flat stones, I thought it might be fun to sit in the dinghy. I pulled the craft to the jetty and climbed aboard, then let it drift with the slight breeze until it was at the full extent of the mooring rope, some ten or twelve feet from the jetty.

I realised that not all the mooring rope was utilised, so by undoing a few knots I could use its full length. This allowed me to drift about twenty feet or so out into the lake. This was much better. I pulled myself back to the jetty a few times and then let the boat drift back to the end of it rope, but decided it would be better to row those few yards back to shore.

To stop non-patrons availing themselves of the boats, the rowlocks were always removed and kept at hotel reception. My father the previous year, rather than have his fishing expedition delayed by a hunt for misplaced rowlocks, cut two short sticks from a nearby tree, which after a little whittling with a penknife, fitted the rowlock hole and enabled the oars to be pulled against.

Back on shore I found a tree with branches of a suitable diameter for temporary rowlocks. After some work with my trusty penknife, the two pieces of tree were fitted into the rowlock locations. A quick test with the oars proved satisfactory. So the new game was to allow the dinghy to drift with wind and water to the full extent of its mooring rope, then row back to the small jetty. This was good fun for a while, but just wasn't quite enough.

Eager for more, I untied the dinghy from the jetty and rowed into the wind and flow for about twenty yards. Then keeping near to the lakeside I would drift back to the jetty. This was much more fun, so I decided to row further out into the lake. On about my tenth voyage, when about twenty-five yards from shore, I turned the boat about and made back to the jetty. Unfortunately one of sticks acting as makeshift rowlock broke!

Being unable to do more than row around in circles, I tried using one oar as a paddle, taking a few strokes each side. This proved very unsuccessful against the increasing wind, which was now taking me away from the jetty and down the lake at an alarming rate. Panic now set in! I abandoned my paddling and concentrated on trying to get the broken bit of the stick out of the rowlock fitting and the other half back in.

I briefly considered abandoning ship and swimming for it, but the thought of the ensuing wrath from parents and hotel owner was a burden too heavy to bear. Being further from the shore the wind became stronger as dark storm clouds gathered overhead. I was now drifting backwards and with gathering pace, getting ever nearer the bottom end of the lake.

I could now see white water caused by the lake rushing angrily over large boulders as it became the out flowing river. I didn't like the idea of chancing those rapids with only one oar. As if by divine intervention, a small sand bank appeared just off the starboard bow, I grabbed an oar and by frantically paddling, managed to run the boat aground. With great relief I jumped ashore and pulled the boat a couple of yards up onto the sand.

My newfound sanctuary was a small island of sand and small stones, about twelve feet in diameter and only six inches above the water level. Although I was still a good distance from the shore, I was for the moment safe. I was now able to work upon the broken piece of wood in the rowlock fitting. Fortunately a sizable tree branch had also beached upon my island, which rendered up an ideal replacement for my snapped makeshift rowlock. After some intense hacking with my trusty penknife, the broken stick was removed and the replacement fitted and tested.

Back in the boat, I pushed off and began to row back up the lake, but to no avail. I failed to make headway against the increasing wind and current. Again I was being pushed and dragged backwards towards the river rapids. I managed to spot an eddy and possible landing place some thirty yards away, but considerably nearer the rapids. I turned the boat around and rowed desperately across the flow. As my landing was very near the outflowing river, I knew I only had one chance. Rowing with all my might, I made it to shore and drove the boat hard aground. Grabbing the painter in one hand I leaped for the muddy bank.

Once I left the boat it was immediately taken away from my landing spot, but not before I managed a couple of hitches of the painter around a sizable willow. Safe upon somewhat boggy dry land, the feeling of panic was slowly being replaced by building euphoria. I had overcome raging oceans, hurricanes and despicable perils of the deep. A quick look around established that I only had to negotiate a short distance of bog to reach the stone wall running along the lakeside road.

I clambered over the stone wall and jumped down on the tarmac road, feeling invincible. I started back towards the hotel, when massive panic set in once more. I had expected a hero's welcome upon my return, when realisation of the true situation began to dawn. I needed some quick thinking to fabricate a believable solution as to how the dinghy ended up tied to a bush some considerable distance from its mooring.

I mentally ran through all the plausible scenarios, eventually opting for the half-truth of that when playing in the boat the painter came untied, allowing the dinghy to drift off down the lake. However, against raging wind and tide I managed to make for the shore and saved the boat. Happy once more with my account of the situation, I continued to amble my way back.

Then on the other side of the road, I noticed a moving mound. Closer inspection proved the small moving hill to be a massive anthill. This was amazing. I had seen ants coming and going from holes in the ground, but never thousands upon thousands in such an orderly mass. I found a suitable observation point and sat mesmerised by the endeavour and purpose of these industrious insects. Of course I had no idea of the time or how long I had been missing. With my preoccupation I had never given the passage of time one thought.

Meanwhile, it had been decided that the family would visit the early evening cinema in the nearby town of Keswick. Unable to find me inside the hotel, Mother despatched my adult brother to search the grounds. Apparently my brother's efforts led him down to the lake where he noted that one of the boats was missing. After half an hour of fruitless search, my brother returned to the hotel. As a boat was missing, he asked the hotel receptionist who had taken it out, thinking that I may have gone with him or them.

Eventually it dawned upon my family and hotel staff that it was probably me who had taken the boat and I was by now drowned somewhere. The pending storm finally broke as my father and brother reached the remaining boat beached near the jetty. Quickly they had the craft in the water and typically my father took the oars. Before they had gone more than a few yards they realised that the boat was filling with water rapidly. In addition to the downpour, the boat had a serious leak which my brother although bailing madly could barely keep at bay.

With the fading light and increasing rain, I reluctantly left my ant hill and hurried up the road towards our hotel. Entering the main door, I was immediately pounced upon by equally anxious mother, sister and hotel staff. I pleaded my rehearsed defence to little effect and was unfairly I thought, banished to bed without my evening meal or visit to the cinema.

It was some two hours later or more and in total darkness that my exhausted and half drowned father and brother returned. I would discover sometime later that the pair had to be physically restrained from dragging me from my room and actually drowning me in the lake.

It was all very unfair. I was the one who had shown ingenuity, great courage and seamanship in the face of adversity and had to spend the next six months 'in disgrace' as my mother termed it. On the other hand, my father and brother would at every opportunity recount their tale of heroic 'derring-do' in overcoming hurricanes and tempests while affecting a dangerous rescue in a sinking boat.

Once relative calm had been restored, my family without me went off to Keswick to catch the later film showing. Shortly afterwards a lady member of the hotel staff knocked upon my door. This kindly lady hearing that I was being deprived of sustenance as punishment, turned up with a glass of milk and a plate of ham sandwiches.

By my early teens the family gained a ply sailing dinghy which served to provide my friends and I with many adventures. My fascination with water would persist to my more mature years, encompassing a good deal of near-death experiences on lake, sea, canal and river in a wide range of craft, whilst also developing a keen interest in researching the industrial archaeological aspect of the early use of water as a power source or for surface and underground transportation.

III

I suppose it was only natural that I should introduce my two sons to the adventures afforded by water at an early age. Regardless of buoyancy aids and life jackets, I was banned from taking my boys on any kind of water-borne craft until they were proficient swimmers and could save their own lives. They were, however, as soon they could barely walk, initiated in the joys of playing 'Pooh Sticks' from the same woodland bridge that I had played on some thirty-odd years earlier.

This particular bridge with open slatted sides was ideal for the game. My boys would drop twigs or sticks from one side of the bridge into the gently flowing muddy water below. Then would hurry across the narrow wooden boards to the other side and wait expectedly for their twig or stick to reappear. The owner of the first flotsam to drift out from under the bridge gave the mandatory excited cheer of victory. This became one of their favourite activities, a wander through the woodland with games of 'hide and seek', ending in a highly competitive game of 'Pooh Sticks', which as my sons gained strength became more like 'Pooh Logs'.

Of course this gentle activity eventually progressed to major 'damming'. I must admit that this transition was not the result of Darwinian evolution, but by the time-honoured method where 'knowledge of the older boy is passed to the younger', with me on this occasion being the 'older boy'. The three of us would occupy ourselves for hours damming up the same woodland stream of my childhood. My sons like me those many years earlier, took great pride in considerably raising the water level.

Of course, we kept secret these activities from their mother. If she ever found out how many times her babies were nearly swept away by the raging torrents of questionable water as our dams collapsed, she would have like many parents all those years before banned us from this enjoyable pastime.

I take great pride in being an advanced pioneer in child development, as only now some thirty or so years later, the ethos and pastoral benefits of 'damming' and flooding vast tracts of land have been recognised as an essential activity for the normal development of children. For at the time of writing, that august institution The National Trust has launched a nationwide campaign *"Fifty things to do before you're eleven and three-quarters"* in order to encourage sofa-bound children to get outside. They list *"Dam a stream"* at number fourteen and *"Go rafting"* at forty-three as a prerequisite in the process of turning children into upright members of society. Had our parents possessed this knowledge, possibly they would not have curtailed our activities all those years ago!

The downside of my two boys' early swimming lessons was the recognition of their potential for development. This would end life as we had known it, as for the next decade or so my wife and I would dedicate ourselves to the daily transportation to swimming pools and endless hours of pool watching. Although many weekends were taken up with swimming competitions or training camps, in addition to the family annual holiday, the boys and I managed one week in early September doing boys' things in the Lake District.

We camped on the shores of Ullswater, which provided easy access to wonderful mountains and fells but importantly magnificent miles of lake water. In the early days we would hire canoes, rowing or motor boats, until eventually we had our own. The first year we towed our own sailing dinghy Mole, which we were able to beach a few yards from the tent. Adam, my youngest, then around ten years old, would suddenly realise that we were missing a vital provision and volunteered to row across the lake to the village of Glen Ridding in order to purchase this essential item.

I casually approved this strategic expedition, knowing full well it was just an excuse to row across the lake. What he didn't know was that I would monitor his progress closely through field glasses. Although he was by this time a successful competitive swimmer, he recognised the importance of wearing a life jacket. It was with great pride I watched his confidence and skill with the oars as he maintained a straight course in a strong crosswind. Reaching the other side he manoeuvred around other craft including the lake ferry and tied up alongside the landing stage.

In due course both boys would be proficient with oar, sail and outboard motor. They would both as soon as passing their driving tests, tow Mole on numerous camping holidays with their friends to the Lakes and North Wales coast. I took great pleasure from knowing that my sons appreciated and enjoyed the natural beauty of the outdoors and specifically water! Whether they had enjoyed being subjected to endless viewings of the "Swallows & Amazons" video is another matter.

Introduction

"I told you I was ill."
The epitaph of Spike Milligan

Being active, of good health and having the constitution of an ox, it came as a bit of a shock when aged fifty-seven, I was struck down with an unidentified illness. My flu-like condition and weakness which rendered me horizontal and curtailed any activity remained misdiagnosed for some eight months. Finally I was referred to a specialist in immunology, who having x-rayed my vitals and sampled all my bodily fluids, eventually discovered antibodies of the Epstein-Barr virus.

Contraction of the Epstein-Barr virus manifests as glandular fever, generally affecting the young and in particular teenagers. The debilitating after-effects may be of short- or long-term consequence, depending upon the individual's previous health and immune system capability, and may return at times of overexertion. As with many other illnesses, the effects may have far more impact upon those mature in years.

So I was finally diagnosed as suffering from PVFS/ME or 'Post Viral Fatigue Syndrome'/'Myalgic Encephalomyelitis' and even CFS or 'Chronic Fatigue Syndrome'. The good news was that my condition at last had a name, the bad news being that there was no cure! The main issue being that although my immune system had won its battle with the horrid virus, it had lost the war and was now in a very low state.

The uplifting prognosis was that my condition may take anything from six months to six years to improve if I was lucky and equally, likely to never improve! It's not my intention to dwell upon my illness, but I would like to think that my adventure may be helpful or even provide inspiration for other fellow sufferers or indeed non-sufferers. Equally I feel it is necessary to emphasise the need for improved support and understanding for those suffering from this terrible condition.

I was lucky to avoid the wide range of debilitating and painful symptoms normally associated with this condition. I just felt wretched and was totally exhausted by any activity, with the only minor relief being sleep. I was surprised to discover legions of people around the world suffered from the same condition and interestingly, many sport stars and celebrities. What was not so good, was learning how many people died of ME or how many times physicians had misdiagnosed or refused to acknowledge the condition.

Life as I had known it ended, including employment. However, the advice for my recovery was to keep active, not to stay in bed, avoid sleep-inducing comfy furniture and choose a hard, upright chair instead. Also to get plenty of fresh air rather than the warmth of indoors. When you're ill the brain doesn't function properly, so we readily follow the advice or instruction offered by those who are supposedly qualified and knowledgeable in these aspects. Needless to say, that by following the advice I made my condition considerable worse.

In order to be able to undertake minor activities, whether physical or mental, I consumed vast amounts of high-sugar-based foods for a quick energy fix. Needless to say, due to my sugar-based diet and inactivity, my weight gain was considerable. As I approached my third year of sloth-like existence, I became preoccupied about the state of my health and in particular, my lack of cardiovascular exercise and the worrying implications for someone in their early sixties like me, especially as my blood pressure had become of concern. Not yet dangerously high, but high enough for my GP to prescribe daily medication. I found that by ignoring previous advice and instigating a strict regime of regular forty-minute sleep periods throughout the day, I could undertake a few less demanding activities in the remaining intervals.

Research also suggested that diet was an important factor for recovery. So I began to overdose on fresh fruit and vegetables, starting each day with the all-important porridge oats. Next I addressed exercise, which was initially limited to lifting arms and legs whilst lying on the floor. This was done prior to a sleep period, to minimise any detrimental after-affect. Walking was still very difficult and any effort to advance in this basic capability proved challenging. I still found standing or sitting upright hard work and could only use my computer for limited periods before becoming exhausted.

We still had all the gym equipment from our sons' sporting era. I decided to try the rowing machine and found it to be ideal, as it could be used while sitting down. Initially I rowed in arms only mode, just one pull on the easy setting every ten seconds. This I did, extending the exercise periods by increments of minutes. Then I included legs as well and by keeping up a gentle pace I could at least increase my heart rate for ten minutes.

With my eventual improvement in health and physical capability, I became able to undertake more less strenuous activities, providing that I still maintained the all-essential regular sleep periods throughout the day. Trying to force my recovery progress or missing a rest period had very unpleasant repercussions.

I realised that in order to sustain the momentum of my recovery, I would have to establish milestones of physical capability for my journey of recovery. Therefore I needed a rehabilitation plan or project to focus upon. Ongoing research also identified the importance following long periods of inactivity or illness, of exercising the cognitive ability as well as the physical. I was surprised how often in my research upon physical recovery, that addressing the 'mind' was considered to be equally important factor.

I was fortunate not to experience 'depression' or similar like many fellow sufferers, but I did get frustrated and seriously 'brassed off' with my limited capability. Interestingly, various sources recommended the avoidance of stress-inducing activities and people when addressing the psychological aspect of recovery.

The perceived wisdom suggested that it was beneficial to avoid those people who had a negative effect upon one's demeanour or feeling of wellbeing. The general advice was to avoid those who exasperated, annoyed or disappointed. The list went on to include those with a 'doom and gloom' prospective, those with an overinflated opinion of their own importance, the self-orientated, the superficial, the pretentious, the unreliable and more. Although strict compliance to this advice would require the culling of many friends and relatives, I could see the benefits. However, according to the recommendations, I should probably avoid myself as well!

Even though I had improved the management of my condition, the basic ability of walking or being upright for any length of time remained limited. It's fact, one doesn't appreciate basic physical capabilities until you lose them!

Importantly, I'd realised that for recovery I needed a project or adventure to aim for, with both physical and cognitive elements.

"Very little is needed to make a happy life;
it is all within yourself, in your way of thinking."

Marcus Aurelius

CHAPTER 1

Just a thought!

"In this world there are people with good ideas and people with bad ideas. There are also people of action and people who just talk. The combination to beware of is the person of action who has a bad idea."

Chay Blyth

One evening I watched a television programme called 'Great British Journeys' presented by Nicholas Crane, the entertaining geographer, travel writer and explorer. In this series of eight programmes, Crane emulated journeys around Britain undertaken by intrepid seventeenth and eighteenth century explorers of renown.

In this particular episode, Crane followed in the footsteps of William Gilpin, the Anglican cleric, accomplished writer and artist who amongst other things it is believed, first formerly defined the term 'picturesque' as "that kind of beauty which is agreeable in a picture". Using Gilpin's own work of 1770 *Observations on the River Wye* as a guide, Crane navigated the Wye, visiting the various locations mentioned. He went on to explain how the collection of panoramic views, the ruined abbey and castles along the Wye, met the prerequisites for consideration as 'picturesque'.

I knew little of the Wye, apart from observing it at various times of my life, as it passed through the exceedingly pleasant countryside of the Welsh and English border counties of Herefordshire, Gloucestershire and Monmouthshire. However, Crane's programme had stimulated my imagination and slowly visions of me on a river, leisurely drifting through the wilderness and cooking in the great outdoors began to form in my mind's eye. I was quite euphoric. This was something that I could do, as it could all be done sitting down!

I had firmly placed the Wye at the top of the list of rivers worthy of further consideration for some yet unformulated project. The two things that my project would involve I decided were water and my nine-foot, fibreglass sailing dinghy 'Mole'. After much deliberation, I had discounted both kayaks and Canadian canoes as suitable vessels. I was fully aware of the safety implications of such craft in the hands of the inexperienced (me) on fast-flowing rivers. Whereas 'Mole' in rowing mode would be extremely difficult to upturn and being double skinned, with vast amounts of built-in buoyancy, was unsinkable. Most importantly, Mole with a few minor changes to his standard strap-style seating would allow me lie flat out to take my obligatory rest or sleep periods at will.

Mole's cargo carrying capacity was equal to the average canoe, enabling the carriage of all those little extras which can convert a camping trip from a matter of survival to a pleasant experience. Also I envisaged just beaching Mole at some riverside campsite and setting up camp within a pace or two.

I had also purchased Tom Fort's excellent book *Downstream – Across England in a Punt*, where he details his experiences of punting along the River Trent. Tom interleaves his daily trials and tribulations with fascinating "exploration of the historical, geographical, social and industrial aspects of a river filled with curiosity". Initially he had also considered the Wye, but had reservations about navigating the upper reaches. Equally he believed Robert Gibbins had already done an excellent job in describing the Wye in his 1943 book *Coming Down the Wye*. Myself, I found this work made for interesting reading about life along the Wye valley, as did P Bonthron's *My Holidays on Inland Waterways* of 1916, but neither provided insight into present-day journeying along the river.

Tom also thought long and hard about the type of craft he would need for his journey and settled upon a fifteen-foot purpose-built punt, which he named Trent Otter. Interestingly, Tom's most important requirement for Trent Otter was for the design to be right for the river, being both "aesthetically and philosophically" correct. This I would come to understand as Mole's brilliant white and blue fibreglass by any measure looked out of place everywhere.

With its shallow draught, the punt was ideal for the upper reaches and could be propelled along with a pole. In deeper water oars were employed. Trent Otter carried all Tom's camping gear and supplies without a hitch; being flat bottomed it was also very stable. Unfortunately, the small gunnels made the punt totally unsuitable for where the Trent became tidal or coping with the wake from constant commercial barge traffic. The weir and locks were also a daunting prospect. So sensibly Tom ended his considerable journey alive at Cromwell lock, below Newark-on-Trent.

Obviously for centuries the Trent had been a main means of transportation and spawned many major industrial towns and villages along its length. Although the Trent would facilitate a 107-mile voyage and does pass through some very pleasant countryside, I wanted my adventure to be more like Huckleberry Finn and Jim's raft journey along the Mississippi, full of adventure but free from urban sprawl and industrial dereliction.

I read a number of informative accounts upon paddling the great Father Thames, which included rereading Jerome K Jerome's *Three Men in a Boat*. Not that I expected Jerome's 1889 comical account of paddling from Kingston to Oxford be of any practical use, but it did set the tone for my own adventure. I had also watched the repeated TV series of the BBC's 2005 re-enactment of Three Men in a Boat with Griff Rhys Jones and co., which although amusing provided little practical insight into journeying along the Thames.

More serious research proved the Thames to have ample camp sites and accommodation, with splendid riverside pubs and cafés etc. Also, I felt there would be an air of dignity and serenity about a journey down this historic river and when asked what I was about, I could claim to be following in the wake of J K Jerome's expedition of 1889. I would of course go in the other direction, as I would need the assistance of the flow.

However in the final analysis, I had to discount the Thames due to the campsites being too far apart and the sheer number of locks, thirty in all. The locks are manned within normal working hours, but upon a late arrival I would be required to operate the lock gates myself whilst pulling Mole through on a long rope. This would not only take ages but would probably be beyond my physical capabilities.

Also, the delay caused by passing through so many locks, would require a generally higher rowing speed. I know locks are nothing to athletic canoeists, who 'portage' or carry their craft and gear up and around the locks and are therefore a mere inconvenience.

The River Severn offered a promising 130 miles of canoe touring from Welshpool to Gloucester. There appeared to be sufficient campsites and accommodation, but again I would be scuppered by locks and weirs. In my final analysis I concluded that the Severn was too serious a river and would not tolerate fools. I had witnessed the power of the Severn first hand and had some experience in various crafts at different places along its length. I admit to feeling intimidated by the Severn and decided that it was just not suitable to be rowed in a dinghy for a two-week adventure by someone of questionable health. Also, I felt that the Severn ran through too many sizeable towns for my requirement. However, I had decided that the Severn like the Trent and Thames would be a must for some future more strenuous expedition.

My attention turned again to the River Wye. I ordered and received a copy of 'Wye Canoe? Canoeist's guide to the River Wye' published by the Environment Agency Wales. This is an excellent publication and a must for anyone planning a journey down the Wye. The guide covers the 104-mile stretch from Glasebury to Chepstow, where the Wye joins the mighty River Severn and provides both maps/map references and details all hazards, natural features, towns, villages, campsites, accommodation, facilities and shops etc. Importantly for me, the guide supplied the distances between each village, bridge or landmark.

The internet provides a wealth of information on the Wye. In addition to the dedicated 'wyenot.com' site, the 'Song of the Paddle' website is where many previous Wye travellers have posted very descriptive word and picture journals of their journeys. I think it was from the experiences of these worthy riparians that I gained the confidence to believe that I could navigate 104 miles of the glorious river. So I had identified a project which would maintain my rehabilitation process, requiring both cognitive and physical exercise in both planning and execution.

I had established the 'Who, What and Why' of my project. The 'Who' being me, the 'What' being a boat journey down the River Wye and the 'Why' for my health benefit and adventure. This left the all-important 'When'. Although the warmer summer months of July and August would be the obvious choice, they were of course the most popular time for using the river, campsites and accommodation hence would be too busy for my liking. The other negative aspect of the summer months was the lower water level. Mole, being part sailing boat, is not flat bottomed and has a keel moulding of three inches running from stem to stern and with the additional weight of supplies and camping gear etc., is not of shallow draught like a canoe and likely to 'bottom' in low water.

The Wye seems to suffer from an ironic scenario when it comes to summer and water levels. In the drier months the water level is low. Also in these drier months, more water for drinking and agricultural use is required and therefore drawn from the Wye. This in turn reduces the water level even further. So if the winter and spring months haven't provided enough rain to saturate the Plynlimon range of the Cambrian Mountains, the Wye becomes low and gentle in its meander to the River Severn. However, in times of monsoon-type weather, the Wye is a different animal, with flood and flashing white water at every turn.

So I decided my 'When' would start in the last week in May. From this point I believed the weather should be both reasonable and early enough in the year for the river to have sufficient depth of water. At this stage I still had no idea how long this adventure would take. From research I knew experienced touring canoeists easily travelled twenty miles a day, although the canoe hire centres advised inexperienced paddlers not to attempt more than twelve. Somehow I had to estimate my daily mileage.

I had always expected to rely upon the current to assist my passage, so perhaps knowing the speed of the flow would make my assumptions more realistic. I contacted Pam Bell, the Regional Officer of the Welsh Canoeing Association. This very kind and helpful lady listened patiently as I explained my tentative plan and was very supportive. Pam suggested that I should in late May with normal rain fall, expect an average flow rate of somewhere between two and four miles per hour.

The 'Wye Canoe?' publication had warned that the end of my journey could be perilous, specifically the last twelve tidal miles from Brockweir to Chepstow. Not only were canoeists not recommended to pass Chepstow as the junction with the River Severn has very dangerous currents, but the guide also warned of the problems of leaving the river at Chepstow due to dangerous soft mud. So I questioned Pam Bell upon these issues.

It seemed that in the main, canoeists avoided travelling all the way to Chepstow due to the problems of tide times and thick mud. Most organised canoeing groups, it appeared, end their journeys at Brockweir Quay as it is the last practical place for extracting canoes and canoeists. Apparently judging the tide height and times was crucial, as trying to leave Brockweir upon an incoming tide would be impossible, due to its speed and power. Arriving at Chepstow at the height of an ebbing tide would risk being dragged out into the River Severn, Bristol Channel and beyond. Equally arriving too late at low water, would make leaving the river impossible due to having a considerable distance of deep, soft mud to cross in order to make the bank.

I must admit to my increasing anxiety about arriving at Chepstow. The 'Wye Canoe?' guide stated that landing was made on "a slipway near the Boat Inn". By using Google Earth I was able to see the aforesaid 'slipway', which led up from the river to a set of heavy wooden gates. I presumed these substantial gates set in the riverside wall were for either keeping back the river in high flood or for stopping moored craft being removed by unauthorised persons. After further research I discovered that the key to these gates was held at the Boat Inn. The Google image also showed a floating pontoon just before the slipway, which could be of use. So all I had to do was arrive at Chepstow at the right time, beach on the slipway, have the gates opened and pull Mole through? I didn't feel very confident.

I decided that regardless of devilish tides and murderous mud I had to end my journey at Chepstow. Chepstow was the recognised end of the Wye, to stop short even by a mile or two would, I believed, downgrade my whole expedition. It would be like walking from John O'Groats to Penzance, a great achievement but falls short of Land's End in both distance and stature. As long as I arrived at Chepstow alive and was able to down a celebrative cider in the Boat Inn, then all would be well. Extricating Mole from the mud could be addressed at another time, if at all. So I had finalised the end, which just left the start to determine.

Various descriptions of the Wye's upper reaches suggested that it would be foolhardy to attempt passage in a nine-foot dinghy. It appeared that canoeists only became interested in this stretch during winter and spring, when white-water rapids made for exciting canoeing. I also learnt that access to the river would not be easy, with few launching opportunities and prohibitive ownership rights. Of the tales from the web, none of the touring journeys seemed to start higher up stream than Glasebury, so I thought it better to reconnoitre this possible starting point for myself.

The opportunity to do so availed itself towards the end of summer. I met the Wye at Rhayader in Powys, some twenty miles down from the source and forty miles upstream from Glaseburg. It was never my intention to start my epic adventure at Rhayader, I just needed to know the river better and establish the best start point for myself. I drove up Bride Street and after crossing the river I found a parking place a short distance away. I must admit to feeling excited in anticipation of seeing the infamous Town Falls in all their fury. I walked back to the bridge and was rather disappointed to see how little water there was; the Wye seemed to pass over the falls quietly without fuss, almost apologetically.

Back in the car I followed the Wye down the A470. Every time road and river came close I stopped to take a look. The Wye had certainly benefitted from the additional waters from the Rivers Elan and Marteg, but still could not be considered as serious. Some seven miles further I arrived at Newbridge-on-Wye. This tree-lined Wye was a river proper, although still a little short of water. For the next six miles the road and river avoided each other until arriving at Builth Wells.

"You can tell a river-lover. They cannot help but pause on a bridge to investigate what lies beneath, or at least slow down to steal a look."

Tom Fort

Here swelled by the confluence of the River Irfon, the Wye becomes magnificent and is a pure joy to see passing under the stunning eighteenth-century, six-arch stone bridge. On the south side however, large beach areas and islands were exposed. I learned from a passing local that the river was at its lowest for three years. That said, there was certainly enough water for idyllic passage by canoe and even Mole. I could have spent a long time at this spot, which I imagined to be crowded with paddlers and leisurely picnickers on warmer days.

Back on the A470, the next sixteen miles of road and river ran as one, allowing intermittent views of the Wye through the trees. The river changed back and forth from wide and calm to flashing white water passing through narrows and rapids. Eventually I turned left over the rather modern bridge at Glasebury, then first left and left again into the municipal car park. I was immediately encouraged by the number of mini-buses belonging to canoe hire and outdoor adventure companies. It was necessary after a short queue, to avail myself of the public toilets, a facility which seemed very popular with the desperate hordes of wetsuit-clad canoeists.

My attention was taken by an elderly couple probably in their seventies, manoeuvring a Canadian canoe off the roof of their car. I was about to offer assistance, when with slick military-like precision they had the canoe down, filled with necessary kit, and carried off towards the river. Intrigued, I followed at a discreet distance. The way to the river from the car park was barred by adjoined steel gates, one large gate for possible vehicular access and a smaller one for people.

The couple opened the small gate and carried the canoe through without breaking stride. Here would be my first problem, getting Mole through this gate. Mole could on his side, pass through the smaller gate on some yet to be designed wheeled device, but ideally it would be easier to drag Mole on his trailer from car park to river, if I could get the large gate unlocked. On the other side of the gate stood a sign, where Powys County Council displayed the canoe launching by-laws. The sign also stated an 'Enquiries' telephone number which I duly noted, thinking that I might be able have this large gate unlocked.

My canoe-carrying couple had portaged the sixty odd yards of grass track to the river and were preparing to launch. They had pushed off and sped away before I got there, leaving me in awe of their performance as they disappeared under the bridge and beyond. Everything looked right, the river was wide with good depth. Launching from the broad beach of small stones would be easy as it shelved quickly, my only concern would be the steel gates. Due to my preoccupation with surveying the Wye I had failed to notice that my fatigue condition was kicking in, so with some effort I made it back to the car and quickly adopted the well-rehearsed power nap position.

Awaking refreshed, I grabbed my small rucksack containing camera, Thermos flask, the remainder of my lunch and slowly retraced my steps back to the river. I photographed the steel gates and the grass path which ran along the side of the bridge, then various shots of the beach and river for later consideration. After choosing a suitable grass-topped part of the riverbank to sit upon, I drank coffee and munched sandwiches whilst I contemplated all things Wye. On the far side, a group of young girls and boys in brightly coloured kayaks received instruction, in some technique or other. A hundred yards or so up stream, a couple of kayaks just paddled around aimlessly and were soon joined by two more.

A procession of three canoes being carried arrived from down the grass track. The leader of the group, obviously an instructor or guide, had the canoes positioned in their prelaunch positions close to the water, then dispatched the group back to bring all the kit and stuff. The leader busied himself checking over the craft. I presumed this chap would have first-hand expert knowledge upon the Wye and be able to provide excellent advice.

Unfortunately our discussion bogged down. A little way into explaining my intention, the instructor dismissed Mole and said I should hire a canoe. I said I didn't want to hire a canoe as I had Mole. He said I should hire a canoe. Again I trotted out my pragmatic reasoning for wanting to use Mole, but to no avail and so it went, back and forth. I said Mole, he said canoe. I was beginning to think I was caught in some surreal Monty Python sketch when fortunately, before I beat this chap to death with his own paddle the other members of the party returned. I gave up and retired to my grassy bank, to finish of the coffee and sandwiches while reflecting upon the previous madness. Was this chap right? Would the journey be totally impossible in Mole?

Three more double canoes appeared from under the bridge and headed towards my position. The six gents beached, hopped ashore and started stripping off helmets and life jackets whilst maintaining a playful banter. They made for the grass and sat in a circle passing around hot drinks and food. I made my way over, explained how I wished to travel the whole Wye to Chepstow in my nine-foot dinghy and asked if they could give me any advice. Apparently they had canoed all the sections of the Wye over the past years, but never bothered going the whole distance to Chepstow.

They were all very interested in my plan and agreed it would be a good adventure. After a good deal of reminiscing and amusing anecdotes, the only problem any of them could envisage would be low water, causing Mole to bang and scrape along the rocky bottoms. Apparently when returning through the Hay-on-Wye stretch of the river earlier in the day, one of the canoes grounded and would not budge until both occupants got out. However, they were unanimous in agreement that my plan in principal was feasible and if there was good winter and spring rain, then I should not have a problem next May and June. Reassured, I thanked my new friends and bade them farewell.

My time had been well spent, I couldn't see any advantage gained from attempting to launch higher up stream than this pleasant spot known as Glasebury Common. If I could get the larger steel gate opened, then I could back the trailer and car almost down to the beach. If not, then some good friend and I could pass Mole on his side through the small gate, then pull and push him on the grass down to the beach. So that was it, my start would be Glasebury. That would make my journey 104 miles long. I mentally ran through the logistics for day one. First, drive to Glasbury with Mole on trailer. Leave Mole by river. Then drive to Chepstow and leave car and trailer by the Boat Inn. Then get lift back to Glasebury with all kit and provisions. Then set off downriver. What could be easier!

Next on my agenda was to take a look at the Hollybush Inn and campsite, which was three miles downstream but only a mile or so by road. At this stage I hadn't given any thought to this camping and B&B facility, but whilst being at Glasebury I thought I should go and have a look. So it was back over the Wye, then left onto the B4350 the Old Brecon Road and within a few minutes the Hollybush Inn appeared on the left. I turned in and parked the car. I followed the track through the campsite down to the river. The site had a good place to beach or launch Mole from, but actually camping there would be a grim proposition. Maybe a B&B somewhere else would be better option.

"It is like a voyage of discovery into unknown lands, seeking not for new territory but for new knowledge. It should appeal to those with a good sense of adventure."

Frederick Sanger

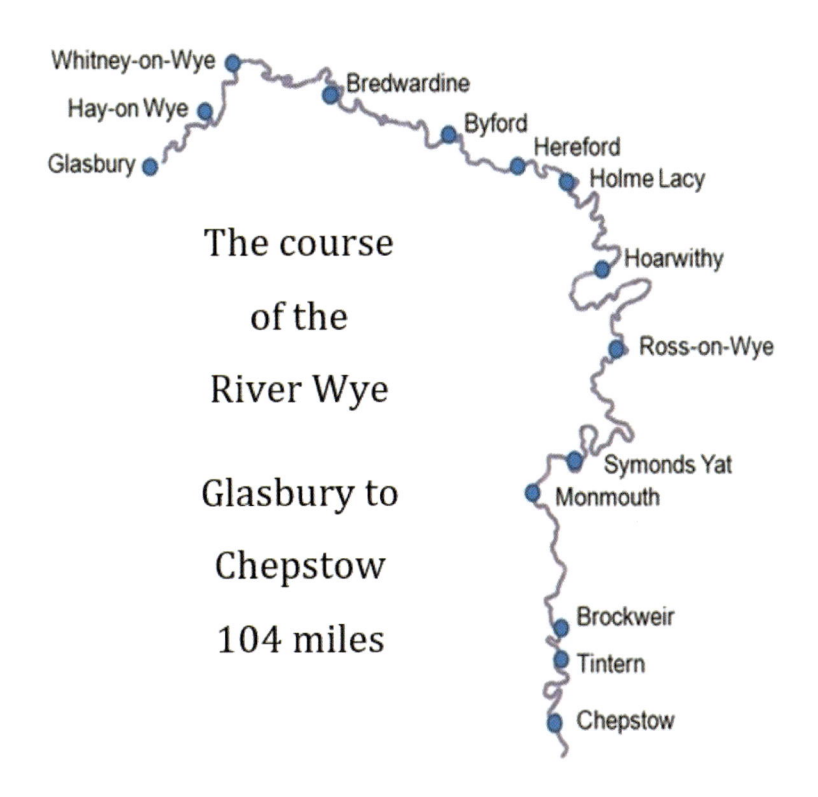

The course of the River Wye

Glasbury to Chepstow

104 miles

Whitney-on-Wye
Hay-on Wye
Glasbury
Bredwardine
Byford
Hereford
Holme Lacy
Hoarwithy
Ross-on-Wye
Symonds Yat
Monmouth
Brockweir
Tintern
Chepstow

Daily distances rowed between campsites:

Start:- Glasbury Common.

Day 1. 3 miles to:- Hollybush Inn Campsite - Hay-on-Wye.

Day 2. 8 miles to:- Whitney Toll Bridge Campsite - Whitney-on-Wye.

Day 3. 11 miles to:- Bycross Farm Campsite - Bredwardine.

Day 4. 14 miles to:- Hereford Rowing Club Campsite - Hereford.

Day 5. 6 miles to:- Lucksall Camping Park - Mordiford.

Day 6. 9 miles to:- Tresseck Farm Campsite - Hoarwithy.

Day 7. 11 miles to:- White Lion Inn Campsite - Ross-on-Wye.

Day 8. 8 miles to:- YHA Campsite - Welsh Bicknor.

Day 9. 12 miles to:- Monnow Bridge Caravan Park - Monmouth.

Day 10. 9 miles to:- Old Railway Station Campsite - Tintern.

Day 11. 9 miles to:- **End at the Boat Inn - Chepstow.**

CHAPTER 2

Make Ready

"Victory awaits him who has everything in order — luck, people call it. Defeat is certain for him who has neglected to take the necessary precautions in time; this is called bad luck."

Roald Amundsen

With the start and finish of my Wye journey established, I could now begin to concentrate upon the logistical aspects, such as what distances could I cover each day? Where would I spend the night? Where would I buy meals and food supplies? Turning again to my 'Wye Canoe?' guide and internet blogs, I began drafting an itinerary. Initially it had been difficult to estimate how far my physical condition would allow me to row each day, but if the river would give me between two and four miles each hour, then I was almost confident that I could achieve the recommended novice limit of ten or twelve miles per day. This I decided would be a reasonable distance for me. After all, it didn't bother me what time I would arrive at my destination. If it took me twelve hours, then so be it. After all it was all about the journey, not the destination.

So then it was just a case of finding accommodation every ten or twelve miles. I had considered hotels, inns or B&Bs. I once had this idyllic illusion of riverside inns, where I could arrive, tie up Mole, stride straight in and being replete from evening meal and odd pint of cider, would retire to my bed, confident in the knowledge that Mole would still be there next morning. I think I only discovered two places capable of meeting this requirement along the whole length of the Wye. There are a number of such establishments set back from the Wye, which canoeist use. But this requires the canoes to be carried or dragged on little wheels a good distance across fields and placed in specially provided secure locations. There is even one B&B a mile or two from the Wye at Brockweir, where the proprietor transports canoes and canoeists to and from his B&B with a Land Rover. Sadly neither of these options were suitable for me or Mole.

So camping it was. It seemed to work out quite well, ten nights under canvas with a day of dinghy transportation at either end. My daily rowing distances would average around ten miles, the shortest being six, the longest being fourteen. The 'Wye Canoe?' guide supplies a comprehensive list of campsites, their facilities, proximity to the river and distance between each. I also used Google Earth as part of my campsite selection process, ensuring that each site was riverside, with a suitable landing place. Due to my fatigue problem, I didn't want to carry my equipment any distance from Mole. Just land, pull Mole a yard or two onto the beach and set up camp within another few strides.

Upon booking my campsite reservations, I explained that I would be travelling downriver in a nine-foot dinghy, I was also recovering from a health problem, which had left me with a fatigue condition and specifically asked whether I would be able to beach my dinghy and set up camp nearby, without any serious effort. These campsite proprietors were unanimous in confirming that this would be so, but seemed more intent upon selling me firewood? This I found odd, as for as long as I could remember open fires were usually banned in all country areas.

My first "What if?" questioned what would happen if I happily rowed past my appointed campsite? This scenario haunted me for a while; the thought of rowing another ten miles or so to the next site was a bit of a worry. Eventually I discounted this problem, as from my internet research many canoeists seem to 'wild camp' on any bit of riverside grass or exposed beach. I intended to be self-sufficient so I could in an emergency camp anywhere and failing that, I would just tie Mole to a riverside tree, cook my supper and sleep afloat. I started to actually find the thought of such an adventure quite appealing.

"I think it's my adventure, my trip, my journey, and I guess my attitude is, let the chips fall where they may."

Leonard Nimoy

I eventually conceded that I would be attempting too much on day one, if I drove to Glasebury, then Chepstow, then back to Glasebury and then, row the ten-plus miles to my first campsite, also I would probably arrive at my first campsite in the dark! So my first overnight would have to be at the Hollybush Inn campsite, being only three miles from Glasebury. It was a big relief to have all my accommodation sorted. I was becoming impatient and wanted to get going, but I still had months to wait.

I had investigated into the opportunity for riverside eating and the purchase of the basic staples. There were possibilities but in the main it would have meant leaving Mole moored unattended and out of sight, while full of my possessions. This is why I decided upon carrying enough basic food and drink supplies for the whole trip and should the opportunity arise to purchase a luxury food item or partake in a local cider, then I would do so.

Now, my attention turned towards Mole. Mole's trailer was in fine fettle, as I had a few years before, taken it to pieces and had it shot blasted before applying two coats of light blue metal paint. I did though, give it another coat of paint, replace the mudguards, inflate the tyres and treat the wheel bearings to a few pumps from my grease gun. Mole on the other hand, needed some serious attention. Obviously his white paintwork both in and out required a couple of new coats, but my main issues concerned the seating. The seating was typical of such dinghies, being of three pieces of board, one running across at the stern, one across the middle and one across towards the prow. This seating arrangement was satisfactory for rowing, but hopeless when sailing or using the outboard engine. Mole had moulded buoyancy compartments which ran down either side, but they were too narrow to sit upon comfortably. I had always intended to address Mole's seating but never got around to it. So now I had impetus to do so, as I would need to be able to lie down and power nap, if and when my fatigue kicked in.

My solution to Mole's seating problem was to remove the original seats and drop in a large sheet of eighteen millimetre marine ply, sawn to fit Mole's inner dimensions. Then with my jigsaw I cut out the fore and aft footwells. This was highly successful. This made sitting sideways and sliding from side to side necessary when under sail, so much easier. Importantly, I could now lie full length on either side of Mole. I also added toe boards along and underneath the side seats, to make leaning out easier when sailing hard. In addition I cut and hinged half the stern seat. This when lifted would allow the oars to be stowed along the floor, but when lowered and secured with a hidden catch made unauthorised removal of the oars somewhat difficult.

I was pleased with my new seating arrangement, although it did make Mole somewhat heavier. I also replaced the wooded transom from the remnants of my marine ply, which along with the new seating and two oars, was sanded down and varnished twice. To ease the pain of sitting on a wooden seat for ten days, I covered a thin foam cushion with waterproof vinyl, which would be tied in place with string. Mole's fibreglass deck covered the forward buoyancy compartment and narrowed as it ran down each side to the stern. The deck's light blue gel coat and become cloudy and discoloured, but a good rub with T-Cut had it back to a deep clear shine. Of course the renovation work took a long time to complete, as the simplest of tasks left me exhausted. Without my good range of power tools it would have been virtually impossible.

My next consideration was how to keep all my camping equipment, clothes and food supplies dry in an open boat for ten days. I discovered the local supermarket stocked a good range of clear plastic storage boxes, with lids that could be secured by clips. After much measuring, I bought three good-sized boxes. Two boxes would fit under the front half of the new seating with the third fitting under the stern seat. These boxes would be impervious to storms and would stay put should Mole be thrown around while going through some serious rapids.

From my favourite outdoor store I acquired two rather expensive dry bags for my sleeping bag, airbed and tent. Although costing far more that I wanted to pay, these dry bags would no matter what, ensure I was dry in bed each night. These cylindrical items would be secured along the inside of Mole by bungee cords. For everything else

I bought very tough medium-sized blue plastic sacks. These I found, by folding over the open end a few times and securing each corner with cord tied in a clove hitch, kept their contents perfectly dry.

Cooking and eating was going to be strategic to my whole trip. For health and more importantly pure enjoyment, it was essential that my gastronomic extravaganzas maintained my high intake of fruit and veg. Although a lifelong baked bean aficionado, they would only play a minor role in my culinary plan. I had numerous camping stoves, ranging from a catering size twin burner to a minute hiking type. The intermediate size models with replacement canisters, had done such sterling service over the decades, but would be a little unstable for my purpose. So onto my list for Santa went a request for one of the new generation flat type single burner stove, with built-in ignition.

After much searching I purchased a small wooden-handled, flat-bottomed wok. This was perfect for my new stove and produced excellent stir-fries, pasta and noodle-based dishes. I started researching interesting dishes that could be prepared with just one pan. I would be visiting Cairns in Australia for my son's wedding in the coming February and so made arrangements to meet up with my lovely Kiwi cousin Sharyn who now lived in Canberra. Knowing Sharyn was an expert in all cuisines, I emailed my enquiry upon one-pan cooking. I heard nothing back upon the subject, but when we eventually met up in Sidney, she presented me with a copy of *Outback Cooking in the Camp Oven* by Jack and Reg Absalom.

The book was exactly what I had asked for, being about one-pan cooking but the Aussie way, using a camp oven! This camp oven was a large cast-iron pot and lid about two feet in diameter and weighing a ton, designed to be placed upon a very large wood fire to cook for hours. The recipes for this monster were equally bizarre. One cannot help but be impressed with the versatility of this utensil, producing everything from cakes to stews and would no doubt in the hands of competent outback chefs, feed hordes of discerning Aussies.

However, I found this book highly amusing and could not take it seriously, due to the recipes requiring such ingredients as a pig's head, a forequarter of goat, two medium kangaroo tails and four rabbits. Every time I got into conversation with an Aussie while down under, I would raise the topic of my new cookbook, thinking that the chances of me sourcing a forequarter of goat would be found highly amusing. But no this was a serious matter; it seemed everyone in Australia owned a cast-iron camp oven and a copy of *Outback Cooking*. These were national treasures and valued processions, which were certainly not to be belittled by some 'Pom'. I must admit, that after scaling down the ingredients of some of the less radical recipes, they were quite good.

I had compiled a list of my food requirement. Perishable items would be bought the day before setting off, the tinned, bottled and dry items I purchased early, as I wanted to see how my plastic storage boxes worked out. I was a little surprised that my tea, coffee, sugar, sauces, spices etc. almost filled the smaller box under the stern seat. I deliberated briefly upon whether I could survive for ten days without tomato, soy or sweet chilli sauce, mango chutney or pickled beetroot? Obviously I couldn't, after all it was a voyage of pleasure, not self-denial!

I had all the necessary clothing for rowing a boat and camping for ten days. I expected to be in shorts, short-sleeve tops and deck shoes without socks every day. My life jacket would provide some protection from wind and rain, which I would wear over a lined windcheater on cooler days. I also took a pair of cargo pants, trainers and a warm sweatshirt for evening visits to respectable establishments purveying beer and food.

To guard against sunstroke, I would take my wide-brimmed bush hat and peaked sailing cap. My only problem that I had not yet resolved was how to cope with storms or all day and every day rain in an open boat. I remembered that in my teens, I had used my oilskin bicycle cape for a multitude of applications. On one occasion, I had used it when Youth Hostelling in the Lake District. It rained every single day for a week and my pals were permanently soaked to the skin, where as I and my rucksack remained totally dry.

From the internet I found an improved modern version. This cape or poncho was made from one large oblong of rip stop nylon with a hood in the middle. Using the eyelets at either end the cape material could be tied between trees to make a shelter or even a small ridge tent and by fastening the press studs down the sides, the material is converted into a cape. The press stud arrangement also allowed arms to be formed, so to convert the cape to a coat, which was ideal for rowing. Being made of light nylon, it weighs little and folds very small.

The only outstanding issue to resolve, was who would follow me to Glasebury, help lug Mole to the river then follow me to Chepstow to leave my car and trailer and then drive me back to Glasebury? Enter Alan. My good friend Alan, who once holidayed in the Maldives and had a personal trainer, has in more recent times been a despairing participant in a good number of my adventures. However, without being asked the good Alan volunteered.

CHAPTER 3

Off we go!

"A journey of a thousand miles begins with a single step."
Lao-tzu

So Monday 24th May, the much awaited and planned for day finally arrived. The car was packed with all my provisions, equipment and all but the kitchen sink. I decided to take every conceivable bit of kit that just may be of some use and would while driving to Glasebury, make a mental final selection of what would accompany me downriver. Mole sat patiently upon his trailer all tied down and ready to go. It was just a case of hitching the trailer to the car, bidding my wife and cat farewell and heading for the open road. As planned I left home on the tail of the morning rush-hour traffic, so by the time I arrived at friend Alan's house the roads were beginning to empty.

Alan and I set about our customary argument over our intended route and to paraphrase Brian Clough, the greatest manager the England football team never had, "We talked about it for twenty minutes and then we decided I was right." This ritual has to be entered into before Alan and I set forth upon any journey undertaken in any motor vehicle upon any public highway. Although we have a shared hatred of satellite navigation and in common with most men, refuse to stop and ask for directions when lost, I will when my carrier pigeon like navigation skills fail, use a modern road map. Whereas Alan, insists upon using a leather-bound road atlas, handed down by his father and some thirty years out of date. It comes as a big surprise to Alan, to discover that his once favoured leafy lane is now a new housing estate or a six-lane motorway. Our motoring trips are always epic and certainly never dull.

We set off in convoy with Alan's car following at the rear. The day was bright, if a little overcast. I admit to having the mixed emotions as I always had in such times. Obviously I was excited about my trip; after all it was worthy adventure to see the much vaunted Wye in all its glory, but I did experience that slight feeling of apprehension or anxiety about the unknown or yet to be experienced aspects of my trip, particularly, the Simmons Yat rapids and Chepstow mud. I had always enjoyed extracting myself from difficult predicaments, but I was certainly no adrenaline junky.

Leaving the motorway at Wrexham we followed the A483 and A470 along the Welsh borders. After the obligatory stop, which all gentlemen of a certain age have to make, we continued on and in our time honoured tradition, exchanged obscene gesticulations at every traffic stoppage. This was not hostility but the way in which we communicated, all was well. At the time of noon and 147 miles later, our small convoy entered the Glasebury Common car park and came to a halt. While Alan went off to reconnoitre, trailer wheel bearings were for checked for overheating before they received a couple of pumps of grease, in readiness for the trip to Chepstow.

Alan returned having considered the problem of the steel gates. He was confident that we could manoeuvre Mole over the big steel gate, providing we did it in stages, and would be far easier than trying to carry Mole on his side through the open small gate, whereas the trailer could be carried through on its side. We ambled our intended route down to the river, noting all the lumps and bumps to be avoided with the trailer. By now there were big areas of bright blue sky and the river looked tremendous. It really was a pretty spot; the river, the bridge and grassy common conspired in composition to which even Alan gave an appreciative nod. I could have set off there and then.

Back at the car, Mole and trailer were unhitched and with relative ease pushed towards the steel gates. With all the ropes undone, we slid and lifted Mole off the trailer and onto the ground. Taking a hold of Mole on either side, we lifted the bow onto the top bar of the gate. Our plan then was to lift the stern and push, so that Mole would end up balanced on top of the gate. Then while one held Mole balanced, the other would nip around the other side of the gate, where he would then hold the balance until the other joined him. Then Mole could be lowered to the ground.

Unfortunately I started giggling which in turn set Alan off doing the same. The more we giggled the more our strength diminished, until we were back where we started with Mole on the ground and the both of us totally exhausted. Our antics had by now attracted a sizeable audience, so we tried to be very serious and then all went to plan. After a long breather, we lifted the centre spar of the trailer onto our shoulders and staggered through the smaller gate, putting down just in front of Mole. After another long breather, Mole was reunited with his trailer and on his way to the river, with me pulling on the towing hitch and Alan pushing at the stern.

After a further rest period and a brief discussion, we decided it would be better to leave Mole a good way from the river, hoping this would discourage someone fancying a little turn on the river while we were away. The thought of coming back to find no Mole, was far too depressing to contemplate. Following many more short rests, Mole's trailer was back through the gate and hitched to the car. Having satisfactorily accomplished the first part of the plan it was off to Chepstow.

Apart from a couple of wrong turns our journey had been event free. A less direct route had been selected in order to follow the Wye as much as possible; we parked up briefly at Tintern to get a closer look at the river. Just over two and a half hours after leaving Glasebury we entered Chepstow, a journey that would take me ten days by boat. We drew up just past the Boat Inn. I walked over to the wall that would retain the Wye in times of very high water and looking over, was momentarily taken aback by the size of the river here, set against the high white cliffs on the other side. Obviously the high tide was on the turn, but this Wye was not the gentle river of Coleridge, Thackeray or Wordsworth, but a powerful muddy giant racing for the sea. I envisaged being swept past Chepstow and dragged out into the Atlantic.

With time I became less overawed and started a methodical reconnaissance of my intended journey's end. The opportunity for Mole to leave the river by the so-called slipway leading up to the large wooden gates in the wall was non-existent. Although once useable, the route was now impassable due to a hotchpotch of assorted craft dumped by the last spring tide and as for the actual gates, they showed little evidence of being opened for at least ten years. Feelings of dark foreboding returned.

The relatively modern-looking double pontoon would be ideal for tying up to and reaching dry land by the steps which climbed up, over and down the other side of the retaining wall. How to get Mole from the pontoon, up the grassy bank and over the five-foot wall was going to be a problem. We started looking for a suitable place to leave the trailer, the car could be parked almost anywhere.

Eventually, we noticed a chap working on a motor cruiser blocked up on the esplanade. My new friend Mac was exceedingly helpful and pointed out an ideal place to leave the trailer. We pushed the trailer into position and then locked it to a metal post. Mac suggested removing a wheel for extra security and as he would be working on his boat every day for the next few weeks, he would keep an eye on it.

My car was also left within Mac's view and having transferred all my kit into Alan's car, we set off back to Glasebury. As planned I entered sleep mode. The next thing I knew was that we were back in the Glasebury car park. Alan suggested that rather than carry all my goods and shackles down to the river, he would transport them direct to the Hollybush Inn campsite and await my arrival.

We dragged Mole to the water's edge; I unshipped the oars and fitted them into the rowlocks. By my watch it was six-fifteen p.m., one hour behind schedule. I moved Mole into deeper water and climbed in. The current slowly took hold of the dinghy and with a pull or two on the oars, Mole straightened up in the general direction of the bridge. I bid Alan farewell and concentrated on heading for the middle arch of the bridge. Once out from under my rowing attained some semblance of order.

Being a nice bright sunny evening many canoeists were on the water. Sooner than expected an island or what should have been an island was encountered. Due to low water all but a small stream went around to the left and then disappeared into some bushes and trees. The majority of the river seemed to be going around to the right. Heading towards the right side the current slowly increased, then as the river narrowed it suddenly accelerated. Everything seemed to be happening very quickly. It was too narrow to use the oars, Mole slalomed backwards out of control around a series of small islands at high speed, banging and scraping all the way. I could actually see the trail of white paint I'd left along the larger stones of the river bed.

This early experience was exhilarating. Now the river was back to full width, deeper and slower. I stopped rowing, shipped the oars and drifted, just giving the occasional paddle to maintain course. I began to look around and take everything in. The quality of evening light was stunning. The golden hue of the low sun gave everything heightened definition, almost a three dimensional effect. The red sandstone riverbanks were home to the countless twittering sand martins, which skimmed back and forth across the river. I could almost reach out and touch them as they flashed by open mouthed, scooping up hovering flies as they went. It was fascinating to see the martins and small trout competing for the same flies.

Apart from experiencing a few more bumps and scrapes whilst navigating a few more islands and shallows, it was a perfect maiden voyage. In euphoric mood I landed upon the beach by the Hollybush Inn campsite. Friend Alan had been waiting patiently with his camera to capture my arrival. We pulled Mole as far as we could from the river and tied him to the trunk of a large overhanging tree.

As we walked up towards the inn to report my arrival and find out where I could put my tent, we encountered an elderly rustic gentleman shuffling along in the same general direction, who enquired as to what we were about. Having explained our purpose, this chap said to camp anywhere and then tried to sell me some firewood. I said no thanks, but would be along later for a beer. So it was a choice of either the riverside woodland where the uncut grass was over two feet high, or a large square of roughly levelled earth with one or two blades of grass, adjacent to the inn's car park. As there was not another soul camping on the site, I did have the run of the place.

Alan then announced that as it was getting late in the day, he would find a nice B&B and stay over. He'd failed to find anywhere in Glasebury earlier, but had been given a few telephone numbers to try elsewhere. If he was staying overnight, I didn't have to worry about camping near Mole as we could use Alan's car to transport all my stuff down to the river in the morning. Therefore I opted for the almost level patch of earth as it would take a tent peg and did have some form of washroom facilities nearby. Alan backed his car as near as possible to my chosen spot; I unloaded my gear and set about sorting the tent. Alan wandered around trying to improve the signal on his mobile phone. The tent was up, gear stowed and airbed inflated by the time Alan returned; he had been unable to find a bed anywhere within twenty miles and had with great reluctance, booked bed and breakfast at the Hollybush Inn. Our thoughts then turned to food. Given the lateness of the hour, we agreed to have a look at the inn's menu and failing that, I could always rustle up a gastronomic delight on my camp stove. Alan said he would rather risk the inn.

Although the Holy Bush Inn looked a little shabby on the outside, it was a good deal worse on the inside. The woodwork was without paint, the furniture without polish and the carpet without pile. I was not surprised to find the elderly rustic gentleman of our earlier acquaintance, now stationed behind the little bar. After what seemed an overcomplicated process, Alan ordered and received a couple of beers.

We seated ourselves. Alan adopted his standard facial expression for such occasions, a cross between exasperation and absolute despair, which I always found to be highly amusing. I'd seen this look many times when our adventures don't go quite to plan. Alan's rules for accompanying me on any venture stated that he must not in any circumstance be exposed to cold, heat, wet, risk or physical discomfort of any kind. Needless to say, I broke the rules at every opportunity.

The beer lightened our mood and gave us courage to request the menu. We selected simple fare, on the basis that it should be quick and importantly safe. While collecting a couple more beers from the bar I tried to order our food. Our rustic host said he would take our orders at the table, so not wishing to break with protocol I returned to my seat. After a good while, Alan called a reminder towards the bar which prompted our rustic garçon to shuffle up with pad and pen. Having written down our orders, he then informed us that it was chef's night off and the owner was filling in, but she was telephoning New Zealand and might be some time yet.

One look at Alan's face had me in uncontrollable laughter. We had already been waiting for ages, so to ward off our hunger pains we had a couple of packets of potato crisps and more beer. I was starting to feel very tired and suggested we should give this woman another half hour to appear and if not, I'd produce bacon sandwiches back at the tent. We discussed the fact that we hadn't seen another soul all the time we had been at the inn, thinking that late May was a little early for the tourist season. Then Alan remembered that there wasn't a spare room of any kind for miles as it was coming up to the world renown Hay-on-Wye Festival, which would be held a short distance down the road. Alan sarcastically added that everybody in the world knew to avoid this place except us, which again had me in stitches.

I ribbed Alan about being careful in the shower, as we were probably in the Powys equivalent of the Norman Bates motel and the lady owner was the long-time dead mother of our rustic barkeeper, in a rocking chair somewhere in the attic. Alan was mildly amused and pointed out that our half-hour waiting time had all but elapsed, when an unkempt barefooted woman breezed up, confirmed our food order and padded off into the next room, we hoped to be the kitchen.

We both sat there, very tired and very hungry. Our period of silent depression was broken by the sound of a ping, which we both instantly recognised as the ping of a microwave. Alan added some highly descriptive expletives about him waiting hours just for a microwaved meal, I just laughed helplessly. Normally neither Alan nor I would have stepped foot in such a place, but when on an adventure one needs plenty of crazy experiences, as one must return with as many amusing anecdotes as possible.

After a few more pings from the microwave our food was unceremoniously plonked down in front of us. We were both too tired to care and shovelled it down. Finished, we bade each other goodnight, Alan went off to find his room and I went off to my tent. Outside the sky was a stargazer's dream, but with the clear sky came the cold. I was certainly glad I had sorted my bed out earlier. I was soon snuggled down in my sleeping bag and happily reflecting upon my first day. It was so far so good.

"We live in a wonderful world that is full of beauty, charm and adventure. There is no end to the adventures that we can have if only we seek them with our eyes open."
                                                                                    Jawaharlal Nehru

CHAPTER 4

To boldly go!

"Adventure is worthwhile in itself."
Amelia Earhart

Awaking early and cold, I dressed quickly and out of desperate necessity made use of the nearby campsite facilities, which fulfilled all bleak expectations. Back at the tent I put my mini kettle on to boil while pulling on a warmer sailing smock, this plus hot coffee soon improved my spirits. Next on the agenda was making quick porridge and as the warming sun had made an appearance, I set up my folding armchair to face the east. All was well in my world as I sat eating porridge out of a wok; the fact that my surroundings resembled a cross between a corporation tip and builder's yard didn't affect my demeanour.

It was time to think about packing up and making ready for the off. However, my thought processes were soon disrupted by two young ladies complete with towels and wash bags passing my camp en route to the facilities. Apparently these twenty-somethings had rented a caravan somewhere along the edge of the wood. They had come to work at the Hay Festival and forgotten to book accommodation in advance, so it was either risk a rather musty caravan or sleep in the car. I briefly considered inviting my new neighbours for morning coffee, when a very disconsolate Alan arrived. Sensing possible discord my two new lady friends ambled off to complete their ablutions.

Having used every possible four-letter expletive to express his utter contempt for the Hollybush Inn and ensemble, I gathered Alan's night at the inn had not gone well. Holding back my laugher, I made Alan a cup of coffee and persuaded him to tell all, having first borrowed a rather rickety nineteenth-century wooden dining chair from my builder's yard for him to sit upon. Apparently Alan was told the inn had been the topic of a recent edition of 'The Hotel Inspector', a television programme which sets out to revitalise failing hotel businesses. Allegedly this programme had been instrumental in refurnishing a number of bedrooms. To the tired and disinterested Alan, the patron rattled on about how wonderful the new rooms were, as she escorted him to the bedroom door. Alan took the keys and said goodnight, finding the room to be nothing special, but was at least newly furnished and painted.

Around three in the morning, Alan awoke needing to relieve his bladder. Turning on the light he made for the door and as the room was not 'ensuite' with bathroom, a trip along the landing was necessary. No matter how many times Alan turned the key back and forth, it seemed to have little effect upon the lock and the door remained shut. After considerable investigation, he was able to establish that both lock and handle mechanism were functioning correctly and the problem lay with the actual door, which was jammed in its frame. Alan was a prisoner in his own room.

With teeth clenched and legs crossed, Alan in sheer desperation pulled incessantly upon the door handle but to no effect. He ceased his efforts fearing that he might break the handle and in major panic searched the room for any kind of emergency vessel or container, but to no avail. Just when he could no longer stand the strain, Alan realised the window could be his savour. Fortunately the window opened, much to Alan's great relief. Of course due to the beer of the previous evening this exercise had to be repeated a few hours later.

Sometime in the morning, Alan heard movement along the landing outside his room and banged on his door while calling for help. Eventually, the lady owner came to investigate the commotion, but totally ignored Alan's request to push against the door while he pulled and insisted he should try turning the key again. Whatever language Alan used at this point is unknown to me, but it did inspire the lady patron to enlist the services of some male to apply a shoulder to the stuck door, finally freeing the imprisoned and very irate Alan.

I was slightly envious of Alan's experience; it had the making of a fine tale, far better than anything that befell Jerome K Jerome's party. This was a much better start to my adventure than I could have possible imagined, especially as it happened to my good friend. Alan still in thunderous mood retreated to his car and read his newspaper, leaving me to concentrate on packing up. As everything had its own bag, box or container, it was faster to do it on my own.

Much later than intended, we transported all my gear down to the river and stowed it aboard Mole. I thanked Alan for his help, jumped aboard and took up the oars. With a big push from Alan, Mole was launched into deeper water. After a few pulls on the oars it became evident that Mole was just perceivably listing to one side, which made him difficult to keep on a straight course. After repositioning my camping gear the problem was effectively resolved. I gave Alan a final wave and set about a reasonable rate of stroke. Earlier concerns about how Mole would cope with everything aboard faded and being much lower in the water, he was more stable and retained momentum better.

Now relaxed, I could enjoy my surroundings. The river took on a grey tone from the overcast sky, but still looked good against the hazy green hills in the distance. Apart from the absence of blue sky, it was a pleasant day, just right for moderate sculling. Trees and bushes began to line the riverbank. Ploughing straight through an overhanging tree gave me a painful reminder to be more aware of what lay ahead or behind me. It was the shock of hitting the branches, rather than the scratches on my neck and arms that really shook me.

Around the next bend a group of ten or twelve youngsters in brightly coloured kayaks splashed around excitedly under the watchful eye of three instructors. Observing my arrival, one of the instructors parted the group to allow my passage. The young canoeists were all very curious as to where I was going, where had I come from, and importantly why? Seemingly unimpressed they politely said goodbye. As I rowed off, the instructor gathered the young canoeists and with all the canoes locked together by their paddles, they began to sing the 'Grand old Duke of York' nursery rhyme. When the Duke's 'ten thousand men marched to the top of the hill and were up' a number of the youngsters stood up in the canoes and when the 'ten thousand men at the bottom of the hill' etc., the canoeists sat down. Of course the ones who were out of sync with the rhyme were 'out'.

I was intrigued by this training exercise. I sculled alongside the other instructor to enquire about this game. It was as I thought, a game to help the young canoeists gain confidence and learn how to balance. They continued to stand up and sit down until one by one they were all eliminated. Through the excitement of the game the youngsters became confident and overcame any fears of capsizing. The instructors gained my admiration. I pulled away and left the joyful group behind.

Areas of blue sky started to break through the cloud, even the sun made an appearance. Numerous waterfowl, mostly with young, plied in and out of riverside bushes, dipping into the river. The only sound to be heard was that of my oars, the lowing of a distant cow and the occasional 'plop' of small trout.

Looking over my shoulder, the river some way ahead appeared to be blocked by a fallen tree. Getting nearer, it was evident that a thirty-foot or so willow on the left-hand bank had fallen across the river, leaving a narrow gap around six feet wide, between the end of the branches and a large beach area of white pebbles. The deeper water and obvious passage at this point ran along the left bank, now obstructed by the tree, leaving only a narrow passage of shallow water to the right. Approaching to the right, Mole immediately ground to a halt in the shallows. Even without my weight, Mole stuck firm. Actually, it was rather a nice spot, worthy of a photograph. Wading around in the water, I tied Mole's painter to the fallen tree, grabbed my camera, Thermos flask, and made across the white beach to a comfortable bit of the grass-covered riverbank.

This was the benefit of travelling on one's own. One could just stop without justification, sit down, drink a cup of coffee and absorb the landscape.

> *"Life moves pretty fast. If you don't stop and look around once in a while, you could miss it."*
>
> Ferris Bueller

It was approaching noon and due to my late start I had probably only covered a couple of miles, so decided it was a little too early for lunch and wiser to paddle on. With Mole dragged through the shallows into deeper water, my progress downstream resumed. Being broad for his length, Mole never did row well. Try and row too hard, he would veer to one side or the other. More progress was made by steady application of the oars.

In one of my contemplative moments, just drifting with oars raised, being taken by the current, I came very near to a pair of very odd ducks, certainly strangers to our shores. They were obviously trying to remain incognito, but their highly coloured plumage gave them away. Like Mole in his bright blue and white, these two looked very much out of place on the Wye. From my photographs, I later identified them as mandarin ducks. Although originally from China, according to the RSPB the Mandarins now numbered over seven thousand.

After a few more rather disconcerting loud bumps and scrapes, the wonderful Wyecliffe Weir came into view as the river turned to the right. This is a very attractive location and certainly was worthy of the 'picturesque' tag. To the left stood a fine red-brick house in well-tended grounds, ahead the low weir drew a line of white water and on the right, the sun exaggerated the white of the sizeable pebble beach. If ever there was a place to lunch, this was it. While Mole hesitated in passing the end of the weir, I stepped out and dragged him onto the beach. Feeling the onset of tiredness, I opted for a quick salami and chutney sandwich rather than cooking.

My bread knife and cutting board performed well. Originally both had been too long for their allotted storage box. Chopping four inches off the wooden cutting board was easy with a saw, but the hardened steel knife required my angle grinder to do the job. That said, I must admit to my bread slices being of doorstep proportions. Even so, it tasted good sat by the weir in warm sunlight. Finding a comfy piece of riverbank, I used my lifejacket as a pillow, pulled my hat down over my eyes and got down to the serious business of sleep.

My little nap ended some forty minutes later. I drank the remainder of the rather elderly contents of my flask while giving Wyecliffe Weir one last look. With a shove Mole was back in the water and I rowed away. Almost immediately the Wye began a long loop towards the left and with it came impassable shallows. Mole ground to a dead stop, so standing up in gondolier fashion, I tried pushing with an oar. Mole became free, I sat down and tried to row and stopped dead again. This method was hopeless, so getting out I manoeuvred Mole into deeper water only to get stuck on the next rock. I lost count of how many times I had to get out and push, but I finally reached slightly deeper water as the bridge at Hay-on-Wye came into view. This bridge with its concrete pillars and beams is entirely unbefitting the Wye at Hay with its cultural aspirations.

"Hay, a town pleasantly seat on the Wye. It was formerly a Roman station and was long afterwards considered as a place of great strength, being defended by a castle and lofty walls, till Glendower laid it to ashes in one of those expeditions in which he drove Harry Bolingbroke."

William Gilpin

I had written a note in my guide to remind me that before arriving at Hay, Baskerville Hall, the inspiration for Sir Arthur Conan Doyle's *Hound of the Baskervilles* was a mile or so from the river at Clyro, but decided it was too far to attempt a visit. According to various accounts, Conan Doyle was a frequent visitor in the early nineteenth-century and became captivated by the hall, family and renowned pack of hunting dogs. Conan Doyle wished to base a story upon the Baskervilles, for which Sir Thomas Baskerville granted permission, providing that the true location of the hall was never disclosed. For this reason Conan Doyle sited the hall at Grimpen Mire, Dartmoor, Devon. These days the hall at Clyro functions as a rather grand hotel.

Virtually straight after the Hay bridge there is a small island with bushes on it. I elected to pass on the left-hand side, with little success. There was just not enough water above the large stones to float Mole and I, so as before I waded behind and gave Mole a push when necessary. Needless to say, walking along a boulder-strewn riverbed isn't all that easy. When I felt relatively confident that the water ahead was of sufficient depth I took up the oars again. I did worry that I might end up walking all the way to Chepstow. For the next few miles, the Wye was the custodian of the border between the counties of Powys and Herefordshire, as well as Wales and England.

I mused upon the conundrum of keeping to the middle of the river, would I then be in two places at once or perhaps nowhere?

I scraped and left white paint upon the riverbed all the way to the village of Clifford. I had hoped to view the ruins of the eleventh-century castle on the right bank, but didn't. Although not much to see by all accounts, it is one of our earliest examples, with a fascinating history. It was apparently the birthplace of 'The fair Rosamund' or Rosamund de Clifford in 1150. The renowned beauty who became a mistress of King Henry II of England.

I must have also passed by the village of Rhydspence as another bridge came into view. Hoping this was my destination, I thought I'd check my Wye guide. I had just read a warning of underwater obstructions, when Mole stopped dead and I went over backwards, giving the back of my head a painful thump on the edge of the foredeck. It took me a while to figure out that Mole had hit some large unseen object. No matter which direction I rowed, Mole was well and truly stuck. Looking over the foredeck down into the water, I could see that Mole had ridden up a giant concrete or stone block. I tested the depth of water around by using an oar; it was easily more than six feet. I did a good deal of rocking from side to side and stem to stern at the same time as rowing, but he still didn't move. It didn't help that the strong current was keeping Mole pushed up against the big block.

I was just about to go over the side and hope that without my weight Mole would drift free, when I had an idea. I wrapped Mole's painter around my hand a few times, so no matter what happen, he couldn't escape. Then on my front, I slid backwards over the bow and down into the water, until my feet were standing on the big block, with the water around my knees. So while bent over Mole's bow and holding under the foredeck, I lifted the bow and pushed off the block sideways at the same time. Mole slid free, with his stern lifted out of the water and me dangling over the bow.

Fuelled by adrenaline I just managed to pull myself back into the dinghy, and lay gasping for breath. In need of something, I unlashed my large bottle of local cider and took a long drink, while making a mental note to in future include brandy in the emergency kit. I set off again towards the bridge, which must be the Whitney-on-Wye Toll Bridge and my destination. My guide said I had travelled seven and one quarter miles and my landing point was at the steps, on the left bank before the bridge. Nearing the bridge, I saw the steps and was dismayed to see twenty very steep concrete steps set into around twenty feet of very steep riverbank. This was the scenario I had hoped to avoid and had purposely asked when booking the campsite, about the ease of getting from the river to the tent pitch.

It took five trips up and down those very steep steps to get all my stuff to the campsite. I was absolutely shattered and very annoyed. After a rest, I went off to the toll bridge cottage to pay my site fees, then set about my tent. Next job was to eat. I needed comfort food, so it would be two fried eggs, a fried tomato and fried bread with tomato sauce, to be followed up with banana and custard and a nice cup of tea. My little wok and gas stove had worked perfectly as did my little kettle. Making instant custard in a plastic bowl and dropping in a chopped banana, made for a satisfying pudding. Apart from the arrival of about twenty youngsters and instructors in canoes, who after loading their canoes onto mini-buses departed, I had the site to myself. Although a small site of two strips of riverside grass, with very basic facilities, I liked it. The trees and bushes provided excellent shelter.

Feeling better, I checked Mole's moorings and sauntered over to have a closer look at the toll bridge. Interestingly, the wooden bridge is a Grade II listed building and the fourth to be built on this spot since 1779. Apparently the three previous bridges, with three stone-built centre arches had all washed away, but the fourth built with pillars of green-heart timber had stood since 1779, but whether it's still the same actual wood I don't know. Meeting the toll keeper again, we chatted for a while. He told me that the bridge was up for sale and of all the repairs it had recently received. I walked to the centre of the bridge and paid my respects to the Wye. A small pontoon was moored to the opposite bank, where a sign announced the presence of a tea garden. The actual garden rose up from the riverbank to a rather nice house, just visible behind the trees.

Upon taking a closer look, the tea garden looked very pleasant and certainly worth a visit tomorrow. I was impressed by the enterprising approach of the owners. What better way to attract river-going patrons, than a pontoon to make getting off and on the river easy. At that moment, a teenage girl paddled up in a kayak and with consummate ease, lifted herself and kayak out onto the pontoon. As she approached I felt I should explain why I was loitering around her home. That done, I asked about the problems of the nearby downstream rapids. Unfortunately, this young lady was of little help as she only paddled upstream and back, never below the bridge. I wondered what perils lay beyond the bridge.

Back at the tent I decided upon an early night, but first a cup of tea and a slice of cake. In true 'Famous Five' tradition, no adventure is complete without a good fruit cake, but I included a nice Madeira cake as well. I also had a large container full of homemade flapjack for restoring energy levels when rowing. Next it was down to the very basic washroom to complete my ablutions. It had become considerably cooler so didn't hang about putting on my sleeping kit and getting into my sleeping bag. I listened to a couple of chapters of *Three Men in a Boat* read by Hugh Laurie on my MP4 player, before falling asleep. It had been another good day.

CHAPTER 5

What Rapids?

"A challenge is an opportunity to prove your ability to yourself, and others."

Joe Brown

Empty tipper trucks! I had recognised the noise that brought me to consciousness. Whilst in semi-slumber, my brain had analysed the nearby racket that had awoken me at some ungodly hour. The familiar sound was made by the bodies of empty twenty-tonne tipper trucks rattling, as their twin rear wheels hit a pot hole or raised manhole cover. I hadn't realised that I was so near the main road and also, where in damnation were all these trucks going to, in this almost continuous convoy? It was only thirty-five minutes past six and far too early to get up, so I played some soothing music into my exposed ear to block out the sound.

Next I was shocked awake by the hammers of hell. The noise was horrendous. Someone or something was banging the living daylights out of a giant cracked bell just outside my tent. It was just past eight o'clock. I stuck my shoes and sweatshirt on and went to investigate. Looking through the hedge that lined the site next to the now busy A438, I could see some chap on the other side of the road trying to straighten out damage done to a large rubbish skip with a massive sledgehammer. Not only did the skip itself amplify the banging, it also reverberated around the Wye valley. Sleep was impossible with that madman at work so I went off to the washroom. I hadn't realised I was camped so close to a main road or metal bashing works, but would certainly amend the campsite's rating in my journal. Walking back I gave Mole a quick look and at least he was still there.

The thought of making five trips up and down the steps with all my kit to Mole, prompted me to make an early start. So it was on with the kettle while I pulled on some clothes. I was poised with spoon over porridge and banana, when it started to throw it down, so retreated into the tent to finish my breakfast. It was still raining an hour later; I had packed everything apart from the tent. My little nylon two-man dome tent was doing well, I had of course carried out the time-honoured ritual of checking that the inner tent was not touching the outer fly sheet, which would in such circumstances allow the rain to pass through both surfaces. I didn't actually know whether this applied to modern material, it was probably a throwback to my days of leaking tents made of cotton-based fabrics.

My next stop was eleven miles away at Bycross Farm campsite near Bredwardine. I didn't want to pack away a wet tent so wondered how long I could delay my start. While it rained, I passed the time updating my journal, listening to my radio and drinking tea. By eleven o'clock the rain stopped and the sun made a half-hearted appearance. I tied a length of thin rope between two trees and spread the tent's wet fly sheet along it, in the hope that it would dry out by the time I'd loaded everything else into Mole. My plan had worked. The intermittent sun and slight breeze had done a good job on the fly sheet, enabling it to be packed up dry. Although I had considerably delayed my departure, everything including me was dry. I took a quick look at my Wye guide, which warned of rapids, shallows and the need for wading would soon be encountered.

With oars in rowlocks I untethered Mole and pushed off the riverbank. I noticed a slight pain where my rear came in contact with the very rigid marine ply seating. I had forgotten to use my specially made foam cushion, covered in waterproof vinyl. This I retrieved from the compartment under the foredeck and sat upon, with immediate relief. Passing out from under the toll bridge, I set up a steady pace. I almost felt guilty about not taking tea in the riverside tea garden, but it was getting late, almost noon. There was some blue sky, but a cool head wind made the Wye quite choppy and slowed progress a little. I thought it would be better to take a late lunch, so to keep hunger at bay I ate another piece of flapjack.

Within a mile of the toll bridge according to my research, the river should be divided by an island. As the river turned to the left, a large beach area came into sight. The Wye seemed to reduce into a narrow shallow stream, running between the beach and the tree-covered left bank, but no island. Whilst expecting to grind to a stop and get out and push, the pace of the river quickened and became choppy, to which Mole responded with an equally choppy motion. Rather than bearing for the stream ahead, a strong current suddenly pulled Mole sideways to the left. At the last minute I realised that the fast-flowing Wye disappeared into the trees and bushes to the left. I just managed to get Mole pointing in the right general direction and ship the oars before we were taken at speed through a tunnel of bushes and overhanging trees. This channel would have been wide enough for a canoeist to make a controlled passage with a paddle, but not with Mole's oars. Mole buffeted from one side to the other out of control with me unable to do anything but keep my head down and hang on.

Finally we were out into slow-moving water and in one piece. Mole established a new feat by leaving white paint along the face of the riverbank as well as the riverbed. Mole when left to his own devices, preferred to travel backwards, so it was as I drifted past the Boat Inn at Whitney-on-Wye. I had originally considered lunching at this proper riverside inn, but decided due to the hour, it was better not to stop and eat on the go.

My reverse passage attracted the attention of a group sitting in the inn's beer garden; I waved nonchalantly as if I always travelled backwards and the bemused group waved back. As Mole drifted happily stern first, I made a sandwich and poured myself a plastic beaker of cider. Taking a bite and a drink, I turned Mole around and picked up the pace.

The Wye began a slow turn to the right and then turned right again. The deeper channel kept to the middle and was easy to follow as the river takes a broad sweep to the left, forming the feature known as Locksters Pool, apparently the home of many sizable salmon in the past. On the inside of this bend is a perfect strip of beach which would make an ideal picnic spot. Apart from a smallish plantation, the trees have all but gone, allowing sight of distant hills on both sides. Large green fields ran right down to the riverbank.

For the next few miles the river slowly meandered across a flat plain and was a pure joy. As the sky darkened, I felt the first few drops of rain upon my bare arms and knees. I was approaching Turner's Boat, a landmark described by my guide as an island four miles from Locksters Pool. This small featureless patch of ground was at this time of low water, barely separated from the right-hand riverbank. Apparently there had been a pedestrian ferry operating on this spot from 1540 to 1900, hence the name. I had intended to snap the commemorative monument to this ferry for my photo log, but dismissed the idea.

The rain started in earnest. The moderate cool wind blew from all points as the Wye continued to almost bend back the way it came, in both directions. I had this odd feeling of isolation; the river ran in a channel with sheer red earth sides of around ten feet. I passed through the countryside totally unobserved and I couldn't see anybody or anything either. Every now and again I could hear a tractor at work in a riverside field, but never saw it. I put on my wonderful poncho, took a large swig of cider to improve my spirits and munched on a big lump of flapjack.

This was a miserable time of endless small rapids and shallows making progress difficult, which wasn't helped by poor weather. Another recurring hazard to avoid were large lumps of stone or concrete tipped into the river to stop further erosion of the riverbank on the outer sides of the bends. It was quite alarming to note how far the riverbanks had receded in some instances, as much earlier attempts to stem the eroding power of the Wye were evident, being made of planks nailed to wooden stakes driven into the river bed, which were now a distance from the bank and a good way into the main water course. Mole loved these half-submerged constructions and never missed the opportunity to hit or try to ride over one.

As we ground to a halt for the hundredth time, I removed my poncho as it had stopped raining and I was getting rather warm under it. Having freed Mole, I let him choose his own way while I poured a beaker of lemonade and peeled a banana. Mole had decided to turn around, drift into the bank and stop. I realised that I was not alone, for just a few feet away on the bank stood a lady and gentleman in full hiking waterproofs who had paused to watch my antics. Apparently this couple from Sheffield had been walking the 'Wye Valley Walk' and had detoured to visit the nearby village of

Letton. They were on their way to see the village church, as it was renowned for being seriously flooded and had a brass plate indicating the height of water in 1795 and one for a subsequent higher flood in 1960. They refused the offer of cider or lemonade, but enthusiastically accepted the offer of Madeira cake.

I jumped ashore with knife and cake tin. My new friends were very knowledgeable upon the area, pointing out the rather pleasant red-brick Letton Court across the field, that had apparently burnt down and been rebuilt in 1927. Also the nearby expanse of water, which had been some aeons ago a horseshoe bend in the river, until the Wye had decided not to bother going the long way round and made a shortcut. So the bit left behind is now referred to by the owners of the fishing rights, as an oxbow lake. My new friends wished me well and strode off across the field; I turned Mole around and feeling more positive, set up a modest tempo with the oars. Once more the river became tree lined and I encountered my first swans, a pen and two signets of undeterminable age. Maintaining a safe distance, I observed these beautiful creatures for a moment or two.

My disposition improved with having only experienced two minor skirmishes with large boulders in the shallows and was further encouraged by the sight of my next landmark; the rather fine six-arch brick bridge, built in the mid-eighteenth century to link the two hamlets of Bredwardine and Brobury. I now knew that I had only two and one half miles to my next campsite, even though it was getting a little late. I had made a note in my log that roughly two miles up the hill from Bredwardine was 'Arthur's Stone', a 5,000-year-old burial chamber. This was just a point of interest as I couldn't even walk that distance. However, set back on the left just after the bridge was the rather splendid Victorian Brobury House and gardens, which I had at one time considered as a B&B possibility.

My good friends the small trout returned with their familiar 'plop'. The flow picked up and I was soon at the next marker, 'The Scar', an impressive red sandstone cliff with large trees growing out of it, which soared to great heights on the left bank of a right-hand loop of the river near Brobury. Here sat some alarmingly large boulders in the middle of the river, just below the surface; needless to say Mole had to introduce himself. Over my right shoulder I saw my first and very orderly apple orchard of Herefordshire.

Then Moccas Court appeared to my left. This impressive late eighteenth century Georgian mansion sits in grounds claimed to be landscaped by Lancelot 'Capability' Brown. My guide now warned of the remains of Moccas Toll Bridge which stood from 1868 until 1960 when it washed away and of course, the remaining stone foundation is still there just below the surface. I allowed Mole to drift backwards as we approached the remains of the bridge abutments. I scanned the river from side to side, but the failing light now made it impossible to see anything below Mole's waterline. Amazingly we passed over the old bridge remains without even a scratch. I was now feeling very tired and regretted not making a flask of coffee, as I needed the caffeine, so made do with another swig of cider. I set about a decent stroke and soon more apple trees appeared as the Wye began a tight turn to the left, then came another orchard on the right which should be my Bycross campsite.

I just managed to spot the Bycross Farm sign, then much to my dismay, also saw the campsite to be about thirty feet above the river, accessed by a very steep metal stairway. Again there had been no mention of this climb when asked about getting from river to site. I was too tired to be angry and at least there was a decent landing spot. After beaching Mole and tying him to the stairway I laboured up to the top of the steps to see what was what. A young chap had been gazing out over the river and was very surprised to see me arrive so late. He was therefore very inquisitive about my trip in a dinghy and when I also explained my annoyance about being misled over the site access from the river, he volunteered to help lug my kit up the steps. This kind young gentleman was one of a party of policemen and one policewoman from South Wales who had canoed down the Wye. The main party had gone off to the local public house and my new police friend had opted to stay behind to look after the dog, camp and importantly keep the campfire going.

I selected my pitch site as near to the river as possible without encroaching upon my new friend's camp. I soon had the tent up, airbed inflated and kit stowed. I was now very hungry and as it was a little cool I was determined to cook something hot. I soon had small squares of my favourite dried sausage frying in my wok, followed by celery, leek, spring onion, red pepper, baby corn and a good helping of soy sauce. I was far from being warm and realised that I was still wearing shorts and wet deck shoes. A quick change into tracksuit bottoms, dry socks and trainers soon did the trick. Next after my wonderful stir-fry was a bowl of instant semolina and tinned peaches, complemented with a mug of hot tea.

Everything in my world was good again. My new friend was sat on a huge log while keeping vigil over the camp fire and willingly accepted a slice of fruit cake as reward for his earlier assistance. He also explained where to pay the camp fees and in the almost darkness, indicated the general direction of the site washroom. Gathering up my wash stuff, I went in search of the loo. It turned out for me to be quite a hike, but was amazingly appointed and clean. Even more impressive was the fan heater that burst into action when the light was turned on. I considered making full use of these good facilities by taking a shower, but as it was so cold I would wait until morning. Back at camp, the police team had returned and were all sat around the fire, so I chatted for a while before turning in. Although I felt ill from fatigue, it had been another good day, apart from the rain causing my late departure.

I woke around five o'clock, very cold and in need of the loo. I could actually feel the cold wind on my face; it seemed to be blowing straight through the sides of the tent. My summer weight sleeping bag was also useless; I hadn't expected it to be this cold in late May. Returning from the washroom, I noted a hunched figure trying to poke life into the dying embers of the fire. It turned out to be the sole young police lady who had also woken up freezing and was contemplating moving her bed next to the fire. Back in my cold tent, I put on all of my warm clothing including a hat and eventually drifted off to the land of nod.

Next thing I knew, it was light, gone past eight o'clock and still cold. I stuck my head outside to assess the weather, dry but overcast. My police friends were already up and sat along the log by the now considerable fire. Apparently they were waiting for the canoe hire company to collect the canoes and transport the group back to their own vehicles. I soon had my porridge and coffee made and consumed it while sat upon a nearby large round stone, roughly two and a half feet in diameter with a three-inch hole through the centre. I would see many more such stones on my journey, seemingly just dumped into the river. I pondered over these stones and couldn't decide whether they were mill stones for grinding corn, or for sharpening farm shears and scythes. I finally arrived at the conclusion that given the quantity I saw and being in Herefordshire, they were probably used for crushing apples in an old cider-making process. I couldn't remember where, but I had seen such stones running around in a circular stone trough crushing apples.

My police friends' canoe hirer's mini-bus turned up and started loading the canoes. The nice young police lady asked whether I would oblige by taking a group photo with her camera. Having ensured she was satisfied with the result I asked her to reciprocate and capture me sat upon the grindstone, in front of my tent. I said goodbye, they wished me luck and by the time I returned from the washroom they'd gone. I thought it best to carry my stuff down the steep steps to Mole in stages between rest intervals. I'd loaded everything but my tent and folding chair, so went off to pay my camping fees.

As previously instructed by my new police friend I knocked on the appropriate farmhouse door, but received no answer apart from the usual farm sound of barking dogs. So I walked around the house to make sure I did have the right door. Being relatively confident it was the right door I returned and knocked again, but still no answer. Returning back towards my tent and thinking the camping fees could be posted from somewhere downriver, I realised I was being angrily shouted at. Turning around, I saw a very wet and very irate lady in a dressing gown standing in the farmhouse doorway. I explained I wanted to pay my camp fees. This lady was not at all pleased. After taking her children to the nearby school, she'd promised herself a nice relaxing bath. Then thinking she heard someone at the door, she got out of the bath and went to look out of the bedroom window. Not seeing anyone outside, because I'd walked off around the other side; she got back in the bath, only to hear my knock on the door again. I paid my fees and said goodbye, only then to be asked whether I'd had any firewood. I said that I hadn't and that the fire had belonged to the police group. There seems to be a preoccupation with firewood in these parts.

Before descending the steps to the river I took one last look around. I liked this campsite apart from the steep steps and it deserved its much vaunted reputation with canoeists. Although it had been rather cold at night, putting up my tent under the apple trees was good fun and the panoramic views over Wye were magnificent. Back onboard and with life jacket on I used an oar to push Mole out into the flow. Opening up my map case, I turned the Wye guide to the next page. Today would be my longest row of the whole trip, being fourteen miles to Hereford. I then had a heart-stopping moment when my guide reminded me that I was only a few yards away from the perilous Mornington Falls. The guide advises to stop short of this hazard and reconnoitre the best route through from the safety of the riverbank. That option was now long passed; as I rounded the left-hand bend the current increased considerably.

Over my left shoulder by the right-hand bank, I noted a small eddy so pulled hard for the sanctuary of this pool. At the current water level, Mornington Falls was a hundred foot or so narrow channel carved out between the riverbank and a tree-covered flat slab of red sandstone riverbed. It was no Niagara, but it did have a significant differential in water heights at either end. This when coupled with the narrowing caused by the channel, considerably speeded up the current. The channel was not wide enough to use the oars in the conventional way, but I could stick one oar over the stern to act as a rudder.

This could go one of two ways, either I would get very wet, with Mole ending up a load of mashed fibreglass, or I would flash through unscathed. I was suddenly reminded of a passage from P. Bonthron's 1916 book *My Holiday on Inland Waterways* where he described his navigation down the Wye, *"There is no doubt that a journey such as this is fraught with considerable danger, and there is a great element of luck in escaping damage considering the amount of keel scraping we encountered even in the recognized channels; consequently none but strongest boats are fit to undertake such a voyage."*

I mentally told Mr Bonthron to keep his opinions to himself and decided to trust to luck. Pulling back out into the main current I aligned Mole to the channel, shipped both oars and sitting sideways I stuck an oar over the transom. Mole buffeted over the rapids as he sped down the channel and amazingly didn't hit or scrape anything. Although it seemed to be over in seconds, it was great fun and I even contemplated doing it all over again. This was a great confidence booster, I felt a lot more assured about tackling whatever else the Wye might have in store for me.

At the next bend I encountered more shallows and small rapids. Mole momentarily stuck his bow on a stone and the current quickly brought the stern end around, which freed the bow from the stone. Drifting backwards, with me facing forwards, meant I could now see the best passage to take through the small rapids. By rowing backwards I was able to get through small rapids quicker and lose less paint. When I came to more serious rapids or hazards, I would approach backwards, and then spin Mole back the right way, as his bow was better for riding over boulders or rubbing along a bank. I used this technique to great effect all the way to Chepstow.

Mole scraped through some more shallows and rapids just after the village of Byford. The trees and bushes lined and overhung the river again and as many roots and branches entered the water, the number of waterfowl increased. I let Mole drift as I washed a piece of flapjack down with coffee. I noticed I was forming a slight blister on my right hand, so rooted out a pair of green rubber-palmed gloves. I had three pairs of gloves of differing weight to try out, but the green ones worked well. Not too hot and enabled me to complete my journey without any hand problems.

Having resumed my progress, the bridge serving the hamlet of Bridge Soller eventually came into view. Apparently this unimposing new bridge was built in 2004 to replace the previous one built towards the end of the nineteenth century, which in turn replaced a ferry. More importantly, this landmark indicated that I was almost halfway to Hereford and therefore, it was approaching my lunch time. I rowed for another half hour or so until I came across a suitable place to land Mole for lunch.

I became aware that my ankles were swollen, similar to the condition I had experienced on a flight down-under earlier in the year. I made the obvious link between prolonged sitting on the aircraft and prolonged sitting in the boat. This was worrying so early into my journey; I couldn't walk the problem off and I didn't have any pressure stockings with me. So I had to be diligent in undertaking regular foot exercises or putting my feet up on Mole's side seating for long periods when rowing. My ankles and lower calves never fully returned to normal until after I returned home, but the exercise regime did minimise the condition.

I dined royally on bacon, tomatoes, mushrooms and a big slab of fried bread. The great benefit of Mole's new seating arrangement was the excess of flat surfaces, which allowed me to use my gas stove and utensils in safety. While eating I set my kettle to boil and was surprised when a chap of similar age to myself paddled up. This canoeist was caravanning downstream at Hereford and as the weather had improved, decided upon a pre-lunch paddle. He was intrigued by Mole and my journey and even more fascinated by my dinghy cooking. I offered my new friend a range of hot and cold drinks and he opted for cider and a piece of flapjack. To stop his canoe drifting off, he temporally lashed the two craft together and clambered aboard Mole. I hadn't planned for such intimacy. I handed over a plastic beaker and a half-full two-litre bottle of cider and suggested that my new friend would be comfortable sitting at the stern, whilst I retreated to the bow.

We chatted about the problems of low water and our experiences of other rivers for about forty minutes or so. My new friend considered it was time to set off back to Hereford, so handed me back the beaker and the now empty cider bottle, before shaking my hand and wishing me an enjoyable trip. I was now tired, so stowed my cooking gear and arranged my luggage to provide a very comfortable sleeping space along the inside of Mole. The sun had made an appearance so pulling my cap over my eyes, I dozed off while thinking about the implications of canoeing back to Hereford after consuming a litre of cider.

I awoke just in time to see a complete family of ducks detour around Mole's stern. The mother duck had four very small, fluffy, light-coloured ducklings in tow, with the resplendent father duck, probably a mallard, a few feet away acting as escort. I kept still until this little flotilla had passed, then after taking a good drink of lukewarm lemonade, pushed Mole out into the river. Although it was a pleasant day I was still a little cold following my nap, so set up a good pace. Large farm buildings appeared over my left shoulder signifying my passing of the hamlet named Canon Bridge, which boasted a splendid Grade II listed Georgian house but no bridge. My map indicated the presence of a ferryman's cottage on the adjacent bank, but I saw neither ferry nor cottage.

My attention was drawn towards large clumps of bright green grass like weed which grew up from the riverbed and extended for quite a length just below the surface. This weed was progressively increasing and ahead it virtually choked the river for a good distance. This mini Sargasso Sea became so dense that it wouldn't allow an oar to penetrate, causing the rowlock to lift out of its socket. I reinstated the rowlock and tried taking very easy and shallow strokes, but made little impression. It was like trying to row across a grass field and without the aid of the current Mole would have stalled. I abandoned rowing for a time, photographed the weed and then sat back, allowing the river to carry me gently onward. It was intriguing why this weed should be so thick in this particular stretch of river and I considered the possibility of nitrate concentration due to runoff from the agricultural activities on either side of the river.

Eventually the weed thinned as I approached the considerable riverside retaining wall of The Weir, a National Trust house and gardens on the left side of the river. Mole returned to his normal self and jammed his bow on a submerged boulder and swung his stern around. After our usual performance Mole drifted free and we continued backwards so I could have a good look at the riverside terracing. A gentleman member of a group walking along the retaining wall pathway asked whether I preferred going backwards. I explained that I could get a better view of things when going backwards. He went on to add, that further along I should be able to see some interesting large square stones in the river near to the remains of a bridge abutment. These masonry stones were believed to be of Roman origin.

Shortly Mole and I reached the ruins of the riverside construction and sure enough, near to the side of the river I could see numerous large but accurately cut stones around three or more feet square randomly positioned on the riverbed. The light conditions were such to allow a rather good snap for the photo album. My map showed the route of a Roman road approaching the Wye from the south east near this point, so I presumed this abutment may have been part of a Roman bridge providing access to and from the Roman town of Magnis, now Kenchester just a little distance to the north, which also sat upon a Roman road running east to west. I pushed onwards or pulled backwards towards my next landmark which was Breinton Common approximately two miles downriver. It was an enjoyable time, with plenty of blue sky but not overly warm. Trees and bushes had returned along the riverbank which restricted the view somewhat, but I never tired of watching the numerous types of waterfowl, large and small, busying themselves in and out of the waterside roots and branches. I was surprised to see a blue damselfly that gave Mole a close inspection before veering off and away, I thought such creatures preferred the still waters of ponds and such. Next two pairs of very serious-looking, camouflage-clad canoeists came up and passed by with little more than a nod of acknowledgement. I presumed Mole's bright white and blue paint coupled with my bright red lifejacket were deemed to offend the serene dignity of the Wye.

By late afternoon, my customary tiredness returned and I regretted allowing my last new friend to finish off the cider, so had to rely upon my high-energy flapjack and lemonade for a boost. I was positive I'd covered the two miles to Breinton Common, but couldn't remember encountering the island as stated in my guide. I heard a familiar 'plop' nearby and thought the small trout had come out to play, when close to my left side I heard another 'plop' and glimpsed a small white spherical object sinking to the depths. Turning around, Belmont Golf Course appeared on the right side of the river and just along the fairway stood three golfers looking in my direction. One chap was holding a club with both hands while resting the shaft on his shoulder, as golfers often do when watching the flight of a ball after taking a shot. My presence must have made for a very tempting target, so to prevent further bombardment I made much of taking out my camera and focusing upon the trio, as if to acquire photographic evidence of my alleged assailants. My ploy appeared to have been successful, as the three bombardiers made off in haste pulling their trolleys behind them. I couldn't be angry, as I probably did something equally as stupid in my twenties.

CHAPTER 6

Boats Small and Big

Row, row, row your boat, gently down the stream,
Merrily, merrily, merrily, merrily life is but a dream.

Anon

Although passing the golf course had been rather hazardous, I now knew that my next overnight stop at Hereford was not far off. A solitary swan cruised by but paid me no heed. My river was of good width and depth as it rounded to the left and then to the right. Trees and bushes still lined the banks, fields and orchards ran down to the river to provide pleasant panoramas. Whether it was a feeling of achievement or just pure relief I wasn't sure, but I always felt uplifted knowing my destination was not too far away.

I was just rounding the last left-hand bend, which led onto a mile or so of straight Wye that facilitated the Hereford Rowing Club, when a young lad in an a skiff came gliding up. After a brief interval of rest and a nod, this Mercurial youth turned around and with effortless style shot back the way he came, making my efforts look pitiful. Next I was treated to an exhibition of racing starts by two girls in a double. I gathered that all was not going well as these two made a number of terse exchanges as they repeated their impressive high-exertion starting routine. Then two mature gentlemen arrived also in a double something. By their red faces and perspiration it was obvious they had put in a good deal of effort. However, these two having turned about, lingered for a chat before setting off at a great rate of knots. Mole was obviously an oddity, probably being the only sailing dinghy to be seen in these waters. Many curious people in a variety of elegant rowing craft came alongside to enquire about our purpose. I enjoyed the notoriety and had a pleasurable time apart from nearly being chopped in half when four young ladies going like the clappers strayed onto the wrong side of the river. They were, however, very embarrassed and very apologetic.

Early evening was obviously a popular time for rowing and canoeing. With such heavy river traffic coming and going from the access steps, it made it difficult to actually cross the river and get to the rowing club. Following river protocol, I kept Mole as close as possible to the right-hand bank, until I was all but under Greyfriars Bridge, before darting across to the other side. It was with some disgust that I counted twelve supermarket trolleys, either in the river or on the riverbank as I approached the road bridge. Later I discovered this contaminated part of the river was adjacent to an Asda supermarket.

After pulling alongside the concrete landing steps, which ran along the front of the clubhouse, I claimed a suitable mooring. I secured Mole by tying a well-practised one-handed bowline, hoping to gain some credibility with this fine rowing establishment, but sadly no one was watching. I stiffly staggered up to the clubhouse and was finally directed through many doors and up many stairs to a kind lady in a small office, being the recipient of my camp fees. My campsite was apparently just over the club access road, next to the river. My fees entitled me to use the club showers and bar, which all sounded good, but I was a little disappointed not to be interrogated about my procurement of wood.

Leaving the fine club facilities, I went in search of the campsite and as expected, it was a major hike for a man of my ability, especially with those large concrete steps in front of the clubhouse. Back at Mole, I untied his mooring and worked my way past all the coming and going craft towards the other end of the landing. This put me at least thirty yards nearer to the campsite. After securing Mole, I climbed aboard and transferred all my goods and shackles on the concrete landing. I decided upon carrying two of my plastic boxes first and staggered up the steps. At the top while pausing to breathe, I met the sculler with whom I had chatted less than an hour or so earlier. Seeing my plight, this very kind young gentleman offered his assistance, along with that of his two children, to transport all my stuff. Much to my great relief and gratitude, with the help of my new Sherpas we managed it all in two trips. My new friend lived locally and on nice evenings after work, came out onto the river for an hour or two. Apparently his wife had brought the children and was now waiting in the car, so they had to be brief. Being granted permission to reward his very polite and helpful children, I funded the purchase of some very large ice creams, which was graciously received.

My thoughts returned to Mole, who was not in the best place to be left overnight. I finally tracked down a club official who suggested tying Mole up behind a couple of Sea Scout whalers down at the far end of the landing. Once done, Mole was hidden and out of sight behind the bigger boats. At least now he wouldn't tempt some inebriated riparian fancying a midnight trip on the river. Once back at the campsite, I had the tent up in no time and started upon my airbed. I hadn't noticed that the campsite was progressively filling up with caravans and campervans at an alarming rate.

Being very tired and in desperate need of food, I decided to use up the rest of my bacon with stir-fry vegetables, served upon a bed of instant savoury rice. My new gas stove had been impressive and a pleasure to use, especially as it also proved to be so economical in its consumption of gas. I sat surveying the ever growing number of caravans, while downing my dessert of instant custard and tinned apricots, then realised that a good number of the caravan towing vehicles had canoes on their roofs. While mid cup of after-dinner coffee, a chap from a recently arrived caravan came walking by, so I politely enquired as to why there was some many caravans arriving. Apparently it was the Caravan Club and Canoes or Camping and Canoeing Club, I don't remember which, annual bank holiday weekend get-together. Seemingly, these pioneers were in the vanguard of the main event, arriving early to erect the marquees necessary to house the various frivolities. I was now extremely tired and felt ill so had to sleep immediately.

The sound of raucous laughter and loud music brought me back to consciousness. By my watch it was almost ten fifteen and I somewhat slowly realised that although almost dark, it was still the same day or night of the same day and I was also fully dressed.

Feeling much better, I decided to make use of the rowing club's facilities and although late would finally have the shower I'd been promising myself. Once outside my tent, I established the laughter and music was emanating from the nearest newly erected marquee, which now seemed a little too near to allow a peaceful night's sleep.

Entering the clubhouse via back door, it was soon evident that some full-blown party was going on here as well. Following the signs I soon arrived at the changing rooms and shower provision. It was very odd being the only person in the large and mainly unlit facility, which seemed to be only yards away from some major shindig. Equally odd was taking a shower while being on nodding terms with every passing user of the gents' loo.

As I was now shaven, clean clothed and relatively presentable, I thought it would be worth giving the bar the once over. Upon leaving the changing rooms, I found the bar was immediately on my left so ordered a glass of the local cider. The actual main party appeared to be going on in another room somewhere, probably a formal celebration, as everyone was well turned out. The younger more causally attired element congregated around the bar. The atmosphere was very good, but unfortunately for me, the music was just too loud, a sign of getting old they say. After chatting to everyone and anyone for a while, I downed my drink and returned to my nylon home, hoping my new neighbours wouldn't be making merry into the early hours.

My new day started just after eight o'clock. I had breakfasted on porridge and apricots, packed up and started shuttling everything down to the riverside. It was a relatively warm morning of blue sky and large white clouds. Ever more arrivals made claim to their bit of campsite, including my new neighbours with an impressive trailer tent. These things always fascinated me, from a small aluminium trailer behind a car unfolds a great hippodrome of a tent. It was amusing to note that upon each return journey I made from the riverside, my new neighbours had erected yet another nylon structure to their camp. In addition to their tent, they added a loo, a covered cooking area, a wind break and two small, odd, tent-like structures, but for what purpose I never discovered.

The dad or sergeant major was in his element and soon had his platoon of harassed-looking wife and three children knocked into shape. Operating with military precision, yet more and more kit was unloaded and having had its identification number checked was positioned in its predetermined location. By my final return, the area of adjacent grass had been turned into a full-blown twenty-first century Bedouin encampment. Equally intriguing was that everything my new neighbours had looked brand new, from their car to their canoes. I wondered if this was a lottery winner living his dream, or perhaps a well-heeled chap who I imagined, came home one day and informed his family that their Bermudan holidays were a thing of the past and it was going to be jolly good camping from now on.

I gave the grass one last check for some missed item and ambled back towards the river. Now it was mayhem in front of the clubhouse, with all sorts of boats being either washed off, carried, placed in or brought off the water. From somewhere behind me, three Canadian-style canoes arrived carried by three men and three ladies. The canoes were positioned along the landing in readiness for launching. The paddlers walked off past me, but returned shortly carrying three sizeable blue waterproof barrels containing all their kit. I was a little embarrassed that my great pile of stuff on the landing was probably double what these six were taking.

Now rested from my earlier toil, I donned my small rucksack and mooched off around the back of the clubhouse. My cousin had as a child, lived in one of the large Victorian villas next to the rowing club on Greyfriars Avenue. I'd promised to return with photos showing their current state. Being next to Greyfriars Bridge it seemed to be a good opportunity to take more photos from on high. The previously mentioned Asda supermarket came into view, which reminded me I needed to stock up on cash, cider and lemonade. My walk although quite short was a little more arduous than expected, probably made worse by carrying four litres of liquid in my rucksack.

Back on the rowing club landing I finally managed to pull Mole along to my pile of belongings and began to load up. Believing myself ready to cast off and depart, I was somewhat taken aback by the strange sight of many long double-hulled canoes being paddled like crazy by an equally crazy-looking mob, coming towards me at quite a thrash. From a nearby boat person, I learnt this spectacle to be the sixty-mile raft race starting upriver at Hay, which apparently ran annually for charity and competed over three days. These rafts, racing side by side with up to eight paddlers, mostly wearing war paint or fancy-dress were far too frenzied for Mole to get involved with, so we decided to sit it out. I admit to having a sneaking admiration for these combatants and was without doubt envious of their energy levels. Although all working hard, they seemed to be having fun, be they teams of young men, girls, old men or mixed teams somewhere in the middle. Believing it was finally safe to continue my more sedate journey I pulled out into the main stream.

Once through the horrid concrete Greyfriars Bridge I was then able to inspect in the celebrated six-arch stone bridge of 1490. I was fascinated to learn that during the English Civil War, one arch had been destroyed by the local people in 1645. Apparently the Parliamentarians had the city under siege and in order to keep the 14,000-strong Scots army at bay, the locals demolished one of the arches. It was said to have been rebuilt in a different style, which I identified as the third arch from the left bank. It seems that upon hearing news of the approaching army of King Charles, the Scots withdrew. My next encounter was three chaps standing thigh deep in the middle of the river, gazing far into the distance. My curiosity got the better of me. Seemingly these three were part of the raft race support crew and were keeping a lookout for stragglers.

Now the Wye became majestic, lined with huge sycamores, beech, lofty elms and ash. A splendid willow worthy of Constable's attention reached down and softly touched the river. Immediately the tower of Hereford Cathedral appeared over the treetops, resplendent with its four short spires. I had always found the turbulent history of this edifice interesting, from its early seventh century origins it had been continually subjected to plunder, collapse and rebuilding. I can remember thinking when reading of the cathedral having its roof stripped of lead by besieged Royalists for musket shot that nothing ever changes, as churches are still having their roof lead plundered. As a possible excursion from the Wye the cathedral was on my list. I wished to see the famous 'Chained Library' with its thousand-year-old books and of course the famous 'Mappa Mundi', the round world map created in the thirteenth century.

I was becoming resigned to being unable to venture far from the river. I was starting to feel fatigued from my earlier short stroll across Greyfriars Bridge, so all my planned sightseeing would probably have to wait for some future time. I was certainly glad that my next overnight stop at Holme Lacy was only six miles downriver.

Two canoes pulled alongside and chatted briefly as we rounded the right-hand bend and passed under a very elegant white-latticed ironwork suspension bridge. According to my research, this bridge was built to replace the ferry crossing and opened in 1898 to celebrate Queen Victoria's diamond jubilee of the previous year. The bridge made for an excellent photograph, especially with the cathedral tower in the background and right on cue, two swans paddled up into the foreground, adding perspective to my composition.

The next joy to behold, warned my guide, was a sewerage works outfall followed by a private road bridge. All thoughts of sewerage outfalls were erased from my memory banks. For me sewerage was or should be incongruous with the beautiful River Wye. With all of the aforementioned passed by, the river turned to the right and we passed under, for a change, a railway bridge.

I was really enjoying my time on the river. Having redistributed my heavier items of kit towards the stern, Mole was slightly less inclined to bash and smash every rock or stone. My guide warned of imminent small rapids and recommend passage to the right, so I applied my reverse technique and in doing so my right became left; I failed to make passage on the right as advised and went left, then stopped dead. Having long since given up attempting to free up Mole from within, in preference to the quicker and easier method of just stepping into the river and manoeuvring Mole into deeper water. This I did but stumbled, momentary letting go of Mole in order to keep from falling full length in the river.

Mole given the freedom of the fast-flowing river, escaped! How I did it, I will never know, but without thinking I sprinted several yards through knee-deep water, then lunged full length, just catching Mole's transom with one hand. It took me another couple of yards to finally bring Mole under control, but not before scraping knees, shins and ankles along the stony riverbed. Finally I managed to climb aboard and lay collapsed, allowing Mole to drift anywhere.

Eventually I sat up and took stock. I had just learnt a valuable lesson and was very lucky not to have Mole arriving at Chepstow without me. So immediately I retrieved a spare length of rope from under Mole's foredeck and tied a wrist-size loop at one end and the other, I tied to a cleat on the stern. In future before getting out to push, I would put the rope loop over my hand. Now I was really bushed, I was bleeding, very wet and needed food and sleep. While examining my war wounds, sewerage outfalls came to mind and the possibility of all kinds of diseases. So I washed off my legs with clean water and applied antiseptic spray to all my bloodied cuts and grazes. It was a little early to stop for lunch, so I fortified myself with half a beaker of cider and a banana, which made for an odd combination.

We continued downstream at a very leisurely pace, more drifting than rowing. This was the only way to see and know a river. My trance-like gaze was broken by a youngish couple enjoying their maiden voyage in kayaks. They planned to lunch at my next camp stop, which according to them, had been recommended due to having a very good café, but in the meantime were very grateful for a refreshing beaker of lemonade. Somehow these two were of the opinion that the Wye was lined with all manner of riverside shops, cafés and inns so didn't carry any supplies, but they would in future.

Shortly after my new friends left, I was staggered to see the 'Wye Invader', a massive Dutch-style barge, beached on the right-hand side of the river. The willows and grass growing around the barge were of considerable height, giving the impression of long abandonment, although the black- and white-painted hull appeared to be of good condition, as did the yellow-painted wheelhouse. I looked for signs of life but saw none. Given the trouble Mole had on this river, I was amazed how this giant arrived on this spot and presumed the winter floodtides must be extremely high.

From my later investigations, I discovered this 1930s Dutch-built barge was 130 feet long and weighed 230 tonnes. Amazingly, the Wye Invader travelled from Chepstow to Hereford in 1989 between April and November. It was intended to turn the barge into floating restaurant at Hereford, but approval was never granted. In 1995 the barge was moved down stream to where I in encountered it. At the time of writing, it is reported that in 2012 the Wye Invader took advantage of the November floodtide and left its position and by the end of December had reached the River Severn and was heading for a dry dock. Also, the Wye Invader is the biggest craft to have travelled so far up the Wye. I do hope the Wye Invader continues to have a good life elsewhere. Although the barge was probably a little too big to have moored up by the old fifteenth-century bridge in

Hereford, I would have preferred it to a river full of supermarket trolleys. In the final analyses, it was a magnificent project in true British spirit and I only wished that I could have been part of it. Of course good friend Alan would have to be involved.

Immediately after the giant barge came a sizable island sat right in the middle of the river. For some reason it was not considered worthy of mention by my guide. It looked an ideal spot to camp, complete with trees, bushes and a nice beach. It probably disappears in times of flood which is probably how the big Dutch barge managed to get past. Now the Wye turned sharp right and was restrained from taking away the B4224 and half the village of Hampton Bishop by anti-flood civil engineering. Here stands the 'Bunch of Carrots Inn', believed to be named after an odd-shaped rock, visible in the riverbed at low water. However, as landing from the river is prohibited, it's a great loss to river paddlers.

Eventually I saw a suitable beach to lunch and sleep upon, but found myself to be on collision course with a family of swans. The pen with her four signets seemed unperturbed by my arrival and continued to pass me by. The cob, however, instead of putting himself between me and his family, kept heading towards me. As I changed course so did he. The last thing I needed was a confrontation with a huge male swan. I remembered St. Mawes harbour, Cornwall, 1960. My father was eating a sandwich when a big swan came alongside our boat and made a grab for it. Not only did the swan get the sandwich but also my father's thumb and refused to let go of either. This culminated in the swan pulling my sixteen-stone father out of the boat and into the water. It would be many years before his thumb functioned properly. However, before this menacing cob got any nearer, I swung Mole around and started rowing away back upstream for all I was worth. Having put a reasonable distance between us, I turned across the river to the far side and then turned back down stream, putting as much river as possible between me and the intimidating bird.

Keeping a watchful eye on the departing swans I drove Mole up onto the strip of beach. I quickly had my last two eggs frying along with a couple of tomatoes. The remains of my loaf of bread was getting past suitability for sandwiches, but made for great fried bread. I followed up with tinned rice pudding topped with a dollop of raspberry jam and washed it down with a good cup of hot tea. An assortment of canoe types passed, some lingering briefly for a chat, others continued on with just a wave or a nod. I got full length, settled down and gave my river one last look before closing my eyes.

A boat beneath a sunny sky,
Lingering onward dreamily,
In an evening of July —
Lewis Carroll

Although rested I didn't feel any more energetic. It was row, drift, row and drift again. The hovering flies arrived which attracted back the small trout. My first heron disturbed by our arrival, reluctantly left its perch and lethargically flew off downriver. The river meandered back and forth and for some reason, this stretch was a popular spot with the local ducks. Eventually I came upon my next landmark, the 'Confluence of the River Lugg' as stated by my guide. Here the River Lugg ends its forty-five-mile journey and joins the Wye just after passing through the village of Mordiford, known for the legend of its dragon and its fourteenth-century bridge over the Lugg, being the oldest surviving bridge in Herefordshire. I did expect more of the Lugg, as it was only a third of the width of the Wye. Apparently the Lugg can be ferocious in flood, but now joined the Wye very politely. The good news was that I had only half a mile to go to my next camp at Holme Lacy.

CHAPTER 7

Four-Star Camping and Beyond

*"Experience is not what happens to a man;
it is what a man does with what happens to him."*
Aldous Huxley

Mole and I passed under the modern and uninspiring Holme Lacy Bridge carrying the B4399 over the Wye to the village of Holme Lacy. Just less than a couple miles over this bridge is the rather fine Grade I listed Holme Lacy House, built in the 1600s by Viscount Scudamore. This imposing mansion remained the family seat of the Earls of Chesterfield until 1909, but in more recent times functions as a hotel.

Drifting up to the Lucksall Caravan and Camping Park at Mordiford, I was immediately impressed by the floating pontoon provided for the benefit of coming and going river craft. Typically the site looked to be about twenty feet higher than the river, but rather than having an almost vertical ladder to climb, the powers that be had constructed a series of wide steps running diagonally up the riverbank. I parked Mole up the side of the pontoon and tied him to a handy wooden post. With some effort I made it to the top of the stairway, where stood a fine pergola with many happy people, happily eating away. Wending my way around this outdoor café I followed the signs to reception.

While handing over my camp fees in the reception-cum-emporium, I couldn't resist my usual moan about my camp being miles from the river, etc. etc., when from behind the shelves of tinned peas and shoe polish appeared a gentleman of authority. Upon hearing my tale of woe, this kind gentleman commanded a member of staff also attired in corporate uniform, to porter my kit from Mole to my allocated pitch and in addition, instructed the receptionist to donate half my fee to the ME Society.

This very nice man wanted to know more about my health, journey and experiences so far. However once I mentioned my first night's campsite, my very nice new friend became very vocal upon the topic of the Hollybush Inn campsite, which in his opinion, besmirched the reputation of Wye camping. Allegedly, the collective Wye campsite owners had petitioned one or other authority, to have the Hollybush Inn campsite closed down.

As my appointed helper reappeared with a porter's trolley, I thanked my very nice new friend for his assistance, charitable donation, and set off to Mole. My very helpful helper and I soon had my boxes and stuff up the steps and after piling it high upon his trolley, my helper led the way to my personal pitch. It was the first time I'd looked at the campsite with its white paint, flowerbeds, flag poles and manicured grass. Very new-looking touring caravans and caravanettes were parked with a regularity of meticulous accuracy either side of the access road, running parallel to the river. To the left a little village of dark green mobile homes sat against the back drop of the wooded valley side.

The piece of grass designated for tents was of bowling green standard and each pitch was allotted its own wooden picnic table with combined benches, the type seen in every National Park or pub garden. I had already noted a sign forbidding fires, so least I would be spared the firewood debate. My helper pointed to a nearby neat stack of large grey building blocks, which had to be employed to be protect the lovingly cared for grass from hot cooking devices or pans. Importantly, these rather heavy cinder blocks must be returned to the stack when vacating. I did wonder whether my helpful helper would allow me to hammer my tent pegs into his pride and joy, or would he produce some non-invasive device to hold down the tent? I couldn't interest my very helpful helper in partaking of beverage or cake, but did express my sincere appreciation.

In almost record time my tent was up, airbed inflated and gear stowed. Two young men and two young ladies ambled up carrying two blue canoe dry barrels, which they set down on the next pitch and proceeded to empty out all manner of clothes and camping equipment.

I assembled my cooking equipment and ingredients and just remembered in time to collect my anti-grass-burning cinder block, so went over to the stack and removed one from the top. My new neighbours having watched me walk past with a giant building block were obviously very curious and upon seeing me place my gas stove upon the grey block, sent forth a deputation of two young men to enquire whether the blocks were available to all. I answered in the positive and warned that crucifixion was the punishment for the singeing grass on this site.

Given the stately surroundings, my signature dish of sweet chilli corned beef pasta would be the order of the day. The sliced red onions and red peppers were soon frying away. Next into my wok went the previously boiled water and instant pasta and stock, shortly followed by a small tin of diced corned beef with a liberal helping of sweet chilli sauce. I should add at this stage, that the total success of my gas stove, specifically its economic consumption of gas, is mainly due to my homemade windshield, constructed from three pieces of sheet steel joined together by riveted piano hinge and finished in grey primer. This basic contraption wrapped around three sides of my gas stove and kept hurricanes at bay.

While keeping the contents of my wok moving around, I noted another deputation heading my way. It was obvious that my new neighbours wanted something or at least wanted to borrow something, as the two pretty young females of the party had been selected for the mission. My new neighbours it seemed had neglected to pack the means to light their gas stove and a sharp knife. Upon further questioning I discovered that my slightly embarrassed borrowers had forgotten to bring a great list of objects, so in addition to a lighter, a sharp knife and cutting board, went two pans, a spatula, two plastic beakers and two plastic plates. Of course I'm sure the camp shop would have stocked everything they needed, but I didn't mind helping out.

I thought it would make for a change to eat at the wooden picnic table and so with great gusto set about my excellent corned beef sweet chilli. The weather was still reasonably warm and a number of people strolled by all spruced up on their way to somewhere for the evening; some smiled, others said hello. I wrote up my journal while downing tinned sliced peaches with wonderful condensed milk and a good hot cup of tea. My helpful helper had pointed out the dishwashing facility next to the nearby shower block, so thought it would be a good opportunity to give my few pots and pans a serious clean.

The facilities block also catered for the washing and drying of clothes and in addition to being light and warm I was treated or subjected to piped music. Having just submerged all my hardware in hot soapy water, the female duo of my new neighbours turned up with all my other stuff. The young ladies insisted on doing all the washing up and drying, in return for the telling of my adventure to date. All four were in their last year at university in Cardiff and would tomorrow start a journey downriver in canoes hired from the other end of the site. Although the males were experienced canoeists, the girls were beginners and a little apprehensive about the fate which awaited them over the next couple of days. We chatted away as we ambled back to our tents with all our pots and pans. Shortly all my new neighbours arrived on my doorstep. They were about to hike the mile or so to the nearby inn at Fownhope and enquired if I would like to accompany them. I thanked them for asking but had to decline their kind invitation, citing the distance and lateness of the hour etc., which they readily understood.

Having stowed all my utensils, I retrieved my ablution kit, towel and returned to the facilities building; warm and musical showers were far too good not to be taken advantage of. Back at my little house, I remembered to make my statutory evening telephone call home to verify I was still alive. Interestingly, almost three weeks to the day, Powys Council had returned my call concerning my enquiry about opening the access gate at Glasbury Common. My wife informed the caller that he was a bit late, as I was now halfway down the Wye.

It was still a pleasant evening, so I boiled my kettle and treated myself to a mug of hot chocolate and piece of cake. With mug and cake in hand I wandered over to the river to check upon Mole. As he was moored to a post beside the pontoon and not beached, I decided to tie his stern to another nearby post, in the belief that two mooring ropes were always better than one.

While returning to my tent, I gave the campsite the once over. It was a very well operated site in an ideal position, situated between the river and the adjacent B4224 road, beyond which rose the wooded hillside to an Iron Age hill fort. Without doubt it was a superb place to stop with a caravan or overnight from the river and the staff had been extremely helpful. However, it was just not quite right for my envisaged wilderness trip. It was certainly better than the other sites I had encountered with regard to facilities and service, but perhaps just a little too civilised. Back at the tent my dreaded fatigue returned, so without delay it was into my night attire and sleeping bag, then I drifted off listening to another chapter of *Three Men in a Boat* on my MP4 player.

The new day began with my statutory trip to the amenities, where I encountered the male contingent of my new neighbours. My two young friends looked decidedly hungover but even so, said to have enjoyed their evening out in the village of Fownhope. I soon had breakfast downed and set about packing up, this time remembering to fill my Thermos flask with coffee. I was intrigued to note the recent-looking planting, running along the facing hillside. The bushes looked to be too closely planted for apples and reminded me more of grape vines or perhaps some kind of soft fruit. I pondered whether the onset of global warming would convert the Wye valley into a major wine-producing region.

With all my kit and caboodle readied for the off, I sauntered over to the site reception. I felt a little embarrassed about asking for my helpful helper of yesterday to transport my stuff, so just asked if I could borrow the trolley. Just like the day before, up from behind the shelves of tinned peas popped the man of authority and despite my protestations insisted that my helpful helper would assist with my stuff and then disappeared once more. Next up popped my helpful helper from behind the shelves of washing up liquid, to confirm his attendance in due course, and then disappeared again. This double act I found hilarious, reminiscent of meerkats, but thought it wiser to keep this comparison to myself.

Upon returning to my pitch, I was just in time to wish my new neighbours good paddling as they carried off their waterproof blue barrels towards their canoes by the Wye. I sat at my picnic table lost in thoughts of the river to come, when an elderly lady arrived. This lovely lady enquired whether I would like to join her for a cup of tea, indicating a caravan opposite, as I had been "working hard, packing all my camping equipment away". This lovely lady went on to explain that this site had been a favourite of both her and her late husband for many years and now she came back on her own every year. I thanked her very much and said I would be over shortly as my helper and trolley came into view. Having explained the implications of my tea invitation to my helper, he agreed to leave the trolley, which I promised to return to him when done with.

My new lovely lady friend Alice hailed from the Welsh valleys. Her husband Evan had been a coal miner and when the mine closed he joined the railways and when the railways closed, he became a bus driver. Alice worked for the same bus company and in time became Evan's conductress. Alice laughed as she told me of how Evan would make up time on their route and if the bus was empty, they would park up in a nice place, eat their sandwiches on the grass and do a 'bit of courting'.

I finished off two of Alice's splendid homemade scones and jam, but politely declined a third. Alice's caravan was of showroom condition, as was her car of only a few months old. Although widowed five years ago, Alice still towed her caravan up and down the country meeting up with her long-time caravanning friends, of which some were due to arrive. I was in awe of Alice when learning she was well past four score years and regretted not keeping in contact, as I'm sure she had many amusing stories to tell. I thanked lovely Alice and said goodbye; in return she parcelled up a couple of scones for my afternoon tea.

Surprisingly, I managed to transport all my kit in one trip and returned the trolley to my helpful helper with much thanks. I soon had Mole loaded up and shipshape and then cast off. Discovering that my thin foam cushion was no longer able to insulate my rear end from Mole's hard seating, the addition of a folded towel seemed to improve matters. I was just about to pull away from the pontoon when once again the river was full of raft racers thrashing by. This time I was able to see these crafts close up. The first had ten paddlers and was constructed from two twenty-odd-feet-long buoyant cylinders with pointed ends, braced and joined together with aluminium scaffolding tubes. The second was of similar construction but shorter, only having two paddlers.

Eventually the arrival of the race official's small inflatable dinghy with huge outboard motor signified that all the rafts had passed and it was safe to leave. It was a pleasant day to be on the river; although overcast it was bright and just about the right temperature for rowing. I did wonder if Mole's outer hull skin had been seriously holed and was letting in water, given the amount of banging and scraping it received. I hadn't noticed any difference in the way Mole handled or sat in the water, but made a mental note when at the next suitable beach, to pull Mole out of the water, open the stern drain cocks and see what comes.

The Wye wound back and forth in large sweeps as we slowly passed the village of Fownhope, with the wooded hillside beyond providing the only views. I had started to note piers, which extended approximately ten feet out from the riverbank, usually constructed of roughly positioned pieces of stone or concrete, standing above the water level. I would observe such constructions regularly for the remainder of my journey. I did ponder their purpose until I saw one or two used by fishermen to spin or fly fish from. The river straightened out a little for a good distance and on my left appeared a rather grand sign proclaiming 'The Golden Mile', a stretch of exclusive private fishing. A few yards further down I encountered a fisherman standing at the edge of the river, obviously waiting for me to pass by so he could continue working his fly. He reluctantly replied to my greeting, but I think he would have preferred for me to hurry on by, rather than exchange pleasantries.

I put a good distance between me and the fisherman, shipped the oars, poured a cup of coffee and drifted for a while, just enjoying everything.

A poor life this if, full of care,
We have no time to stand and stare.
W. H. Davis

Refreshed in body and mind, I picked up the oars and set off again. My next landmark according to my guide would be Mancell's Ferry, which I was prepared to wager would no longer have a boat. Nevertheless, I would be glad to have reached this spot, as it was halfway to my next overnight camp near Hoarwithy. While musing upon ferry boats, bridges and things, I could hear someone calling, but couldn't see anyone. The calling persisted until I eventually spotted a chap near the opposite bank, chest deep in the river. Eventually my brain made sense of what I was seeing and hearing. This fisher chap had snagged his line on some riverbed object and was trying to enlist my help to free it. Initially I was unable to see the fine filament and by the time I had, the current had taken me way past. My only option was to row a good way back upstream, then make a grab for the line as I drifted downriver again. The current was quite strong at this point and I would have needed both oars to hold station and therefore, wouldn't have a spare hand to grab the line.

Miraculously the line came free at my first attempt and the exceedingly grateful fisher chap insisted that I joined him for a drink. I thanked the nice fisher chap for his kind invitation, but expressed my necessity to progress towards my next campsite and rowed on. My next vision was of the nice fisher chap, dressed in waders, weatherproof jacket and hat, clutching fishing rod and net, shouting and gesticulating in my direction, while running along the riverbank.

Unfortunately the actions of the nice fisher chap had attracted the attention of a nearby herd of cows, who had become very curious and having broken into a canter were gaining on the nice fisher chap at an alarming rate. I stopped rowing. I was at a loss to know what I should do to help. Just before the cows caught up, the nice fisher chap skipped down the bank, stepped into a moored dinghy and set off across the river, while indicating for me to join him at the other side. It was now obvious that he'd not realised I had declined his kind invitation. However, it was now essential that I should engage with this nice fisher chap, as his previous comedic antics suggested some amusing exploit was in the offing.

We moored our craft to a wooden landing and the nice fisher chap introduced himself as Andrew. I was surprised when later I discovered that my spritely new friend, who had outrun a herd of cows while wearing waders, was well into his late seventies. Andrew soon had the tailgate of his Range Rover open, to expose an Aladdin's cave of fishing gear and fine beverages. Like my garage back at home, to the uninitiated the boot of Andrew's car would look a total shambles. Andrew cleared room for us to sit in the boot, while explaining that he was a wine merchant by profession and had decanted his latest project that morning. From a small leather case my host produced two silver cups which he filled with pale dry sherry from a leather-encased decanter.

We talked of many things; Andrew was interested in all the whys and wherefores of my trip. We moved onto fishing and I gained a few points through owning a Hardy twin-tipped, split-cane fly rod and reel, although rarely used. We talked of spinners and flies, both wet and dry. I was fascinated to see that my fisher friend kept his vast collection of flies in three small leather suitcases, which individually bore the name of Andrew, his father and uncle. Seemingly all three had been given one of these new cases when packed off to the same prep school. Those were the days!

There we sat in boot with our legs dangling; I listened intently as my new friend told many interesting tales of travels and encounters. It never failed to amaze me how many fascinating people I'd met in my time by sheer chance. Andrew was without doubt one of the declining number of true gentlemen.

I had lost count of how many times he had filled up the silver cups, but I was starting to feel very odd. We talked of family, but Andrew's mood stiffened slightly as he told me of his son, an officer with the local regiment who was about to embark upon his third tour in Afghanistan. However, two chaps turned up which lifted the mood. One chap was my fisherman from earlier, the other being the ghillie overseeing the fishing beat. Andrew offered sherry to our visitors but they declined the invitation. I tried to cover the top of my cup but I was too slow, as Andrew had it filled again.

We chatted for a little more about down-under travel and rowing, but I was now tired and very inebriated. My tolerance to alcohol wasn't what it used to be. I thanked my new friend for his hospitality and agreed to keep in contact. Later I realised that we'd forgotten to exchange contact details, but I made a resolution to seek him out at some later date.

I bade the little group farewell but had trouble untying Mole's mooring. The 'Golden Mile' ghillie, observing my struggle with an easy to undo a 'one round turn and two half hitches' knot came to my aid. For some reason my fingers seemed incapable of carrying out the most basic of tasks. I put what I thought to be a respectable distance between me and my new friends and landed Mole on the first available beach. I was soon flat out and asleep.

I awoke dehydrated and feeling far from well. A beaker of lemonade eased my dry throat, as I sat taking in my surroundings. My map confirmed I was a little way past Mancell's Ferry and as expected it lacked a ferry. On my right the wooded hillside rose up sharply to Ballingham Hill and to the east just across the river stood Capler Hill, a large bump of a hill with 'Capler Camp' an Iron Age/Romano hill fort perched on top and also according to my guide, it hosted "a variety of birds and dappled fallow deer". I could just about see a hawk or something similar circling above the hill catching the thermals, but saw no deer.

Realising my discomfort was due to hunger, I decided upon frying the second tin of my corned beef provision and serving it up with my favourite curried baked beans. I could never fathom why food cooked and eaten in the middle of nowhere always tasted so good. I finished off the peaches and condensed milk from the previous evening with a good cup of tea.

I wandered around my small kingdom of a beach. This was another special place; I could almost believe the Wye provided these little lay-bys of white stones purposely to provide river travellers with a place to stop and admire the view. I visualised generations of long-gone people striding down the field behind to take the long-gone ferry. Likewise I could imagine a cohort or two of Roman soldiers marching up and down the now overgrown Capler Hill.

It was too soon after my late lunch to do any serious rowing, but at least I could drift with the current and make some progress. So Mole and I rejoined the river where it began its first of two major loops. Here were open fields on the inside and on the other, a steep tree-covered cliff rising up to the village of Brockhampton and beyond. So enamoured were the Japanese tourists with 'All Saint's', Brockhampton's late nineteenth-century thatch-roofed church, that amazingly they built a replica on the twenty-first and twenty-second floors of a high-rise tower block in Osaka, Japan!

While enjoying the trees I was suddenly surprised to find myself keeping pace with a couple of chaps walking along the riverside pathway. These two Netherlanders with their impeccable English were on a walking holiday. Apparently, their wives drove the motor home to their planned destination each day, as they crossed back and forth down the Wye. They were very envious of my journey, but I had to applaud their equally wonderful undertaking. The pathway disappeared behind the trees again taking with it my new Dutch friends; I said farewell and set about a decent pace.

The sound of distant laughter and fun and games from behind, prompted a look over my shoulder. Far upriver a vast number of brightly coloured kayaks were plying back and forth. Eventually I realised that I was approaching Carey Islands, a group of small islands sitting in the middle of the Wye. The young canoeists were splashing around the islands and enjoying the rapids in the middle. As advised by my guide I took the right-hand channel and passed the islands without incident. More canoeists were joining the river from the nearby field. As there was a lifebelt on the riverbank and someone camping on one of the islands, I gathered that this must be a popular spot. I had never seen so many kayaks at one time.

Pulling away, I observed the kayaks coming to together and then setting off towards me. Soon the leader had caught up and passed me. From a passing instructor I learnt that the group was participating in the Duke of Edinburgh's Award scheme. I've always revered this esteemed organisation and believe the award scheme should be available if not compulsory for all youngsters. I achieved the Bronze award some forty-eight years earlier and from it gained the courage and knowledge to tackle many arduous endeavours. My group in the 1960s were fortunate to be mentored by Walter Unsworth, the great climbing author and outdoor enthusiast.

The wooded hillside continued for half a mile or so and then came five rather sad-looking stone pillars, being the last remains of long-gone Carey Rail Bridge. The bridge had carried the once vibrant Hereford to Gloucester line for 110 years until its demise in 1965. Such is the topography between Hereford and Gloucester that it required one and a half miles of tunnel and four viaducts over the Wye, to lay the twenty miles of track. Its little wonder they called upon the great Mr Brunel. Originally the track was laid to Brunel's broad gauge.

One by one all the brightly coloured canoes caught and passed me by. Having navigated through the derelict bridge pillars, I knew it was only a couple of miles to my next camp, so thought I would treat myself to Alice's scones and coffee. The wooded hillside on the left flattened out into farmland and the farmland on the right became steep wooded hillside. I was treated to a great drift of fifty swans and more. I seemed to remember these magnificent birds formed these great gatherings until they found a mate and formed their own family unit. Fortunately they didn't seem to mind my close proximity, which allowed my observation of this interesting spectacle at close quarters.

The relatively modern bridge near Hoarwithy came into view, but isn't worthy of comment. However, the charming toll house perched at one end is unique. Its style is reminiscent of a Rhine bridge house, having the appearance of being the remains of a once larger house that had been sliced in half. However, the overall effect was somewhat demeaned by its modern white plastic window frames.

The river traffic seemed to be increasing exponentially, the nearer I got to the campsite. The more serious journeying canoeists tried desperately to avoid family-filled Canadian canoes splashing around in all directions. I spun Mole around and drifted backwards while I contemplated landing at Tresseck Farm campsite.

CHAPTER 8

Italian Romanesque and Aussies

"To be successful you must accept all challenges that come your way. You can't just accept the ones you like."

Mike Gafka

The May Bank Holiday weekend had certainly arrived at Tresseck Campsite. Between excitable children and dogs running around in the shallows, canoes of happy families tried to land or launch. The sizeable grass- and bush-covered landing was equally busy and as expected, the way up the near vertical riverbank to the campsite was via yet another flight of precarious steps. Having selected a suitable bit of beach, I turned Mole around and drove him ashore.

Alighting, I was again reminded by the pain in my rear end, to somehow improve the seat cushioning. Once I got my limbs used to functioning on dry land again, I pulled Mole ashore and tied him to a nearby willow bush. I thought it wise to first reconnoitre the campsite so somewhat stiffly clambered up the poorly maintained stairway. As anticipated the site was busy, with rows of closely pitched tents extending along all sides of the field. Conveniently there was a free space virtually opposite the steps on the far side of the site, roughly thirty yards away. On closer inspection of the pitch, the flattened grass suggested that someone had decamped recently, but everything seemed fine to me so I claimed the piece of turf for Queen and country.

After piling all my stuff onto the beach I locked the oars in the bottom of Mole by means of the secret seat lock, slung the small rucksack containing all valuables and vital documents onto my back and picked up two of my plastics boxes. My arrival at the stairway coincided with that of a mother and two children. The mother held back the children and said for me to ascend the stairs first; I thanked her but declined her offer, explaining that I would be going up very slowly, especially as I had that great pile to transport up, gesturing to my boxes and bags next to Mole. I was then required to provide a further explanation as to why I needed such a mountain of supplies. Without further ado, the young mum dispatched her children up the steps and proceeded to shuttle all my stuff from Mole to the top of the stairway, while her two small children and I carried it across the site to my pitch.

I was of course extremely grateful, if not embarrassed being helped in a physical task by this slip of a young lady. She did, however, allow me to reward her children with a piece of flapjack each and after much persuasion accepted the appropriate funds to finance large ice creams at the next opportunity. Apparently the nice mum and husband had been ardent canoeists since their youth, but with the advent of children the couple had forgone white water for the more sedate lower Wye.

It was sometime later, when the nice mum's husband popped by for a lengthy chat about my trip. He also wanted to travel the whole length of the river some day and was particularly interested in the issues I had encountered between Glasbury and Hereford, being his unknown territory. Unfortunately nice mum was not pleased to find her absent nice husband sat in my folding chair, with a beaker of cider in hand, especially when he had been ordered to undertake various important tasks. The nice husband sheepishly wished me good luck and sloped off in disgrace. I pondered this scenario, for on many occasions in years long passed, I also was accused of dereliction of duty when found missing or chatting with other chaps on campsites. I presumed it must be a wife thing, not wanting husbands to enjoy themselves when on holiday!

Rain clouds gathered overhead so I concentrated upon getting my tent up and goods stored without delay. Satisfied I was waterproof, my thoughts returned to Mole and the necessity to pull him clear of the water and out of the way of the busy beach. Reaching the top of the steps, my heart stopped and sheer panic set in. My biggest fear had been realised, Mole had gone! Eventually after I remembered to breathe, I scanned the whole panorama back and forth and just caught a flash of Mole's bright blue foredeck through the tops of the trees, some way off downriver.

Initially I thought someone must have cast Mole adrift, but he seemed stationary; perhaps he had run aground or got stuck on something? It was useless to panic, but in a deliberate manner I was down the rough steps and along the narrow track which ran through a small copse of willow by the riverside. As the bushes and trees thinned out I could see Mole around fifty yards away mid-channel, straining at the end of his painter. At the other end, was a group of three children. Resisting the urge to rush up and drown all three, I stealthily approached and had another heart-stopping moment when realising the main protagonist, a boy of approximately nine years, seemed to have a very casual hold of Mole's painter. Obviously any surprise or shock would cause the boy to let go and despatch Mole to Chepstow and beyond.

Backtracking away from the little darlings, I noted another small track running parallel to the first but along the base of the riverbank. I casually walked along this new path whistling and looking in every direction but at the three children. Upon reaching the river, my track joined the first track. I was almost level with Mole, but never gave him or the children a glance and after pausing for a moment or two slowly ambled back up the first path towards the little group. As I approached, the boy and two smaller girls shuffled off the path to let me pass. Rather than passing and in a very matter of fact manner, I took a vice-like grip on Mole's painter and gently eased it from the boy's hand. The little group remained silent as I set off towing Mole back from whence he came.

I know I should have known better, but I stopped, turned around and asked the three why they had taken Mole? Apparently, they just found him there; someone else must have pushed him into the water, they just found the rope in the grass. It all sounded very familiar, but I couldn't complain as I did want an adventure full of trials and tribulations.

Back at the beach I pulled Mole as far ashore as possible and this time used three ropes tied with very difficult knots to three good-sized trees. I sat on Mole for a while to recover; my earlier adrenaline-fuelled energy was now gone and replaced by tiredness. Very slowly I ascended the stairway back to the campsite. Walking towards my tent I realised that I hadn't paid much attention to my new surrounds. I noted the odd water tap and toilet facilities provided by five blue portable toilets which upon inspection were found to be just about useable. Showers, however, were conspicuous by their absence.

The small but pleasant village of Hoarwithy lay approximately a quarter of a mile in a north-westerly direction from the campsite. Within my walking distance at the end to the site access road stood the New Harp Inn. I had contemplated sampling the local cider, but being a bank holiday I considered it would probably be crowded, so decided to give it a miss. However, I was somewhat intrigued by the exquisite church of St. Catherine's, with its square tower of red sandstone tall above the treeline. I was aware Hoarwithy had a church in the architecture style of 'Italian Romanesque', but the actual building was amazing and certainly worth a closer look tomorrow.

It was time to sort my evening meal. The threatening rainclouds and the cooler temperature suggested that my alfresco eating may not be very pleasant, but decided to risk it. I quickly settled upon a stir-fry of Spam, vegetables and noodles. I was looking forward to tasting the Spam as it must have been at least fifty years since I last experienced it. I found chopping vegetables and pushing them around a wok very satisfying as well as tasty, but I had to stop myself from having stir-fries at every meal. So it was into the tent to retrieve my meal-time supplies and equipment and having piled my cooking stuff on top of my food box, backed out again on all fours. I stood up, turned around and found myself eyeball to eyeball with a perfectly formed young lady, wearing a very small red bikini.

This blonde, tanned Aussie and partner had set about cooking a chilli only to discover they had forgotten the all-important chilli powder. She had unsuccessfully enquired at every tent in her quest for the strategic ingredient and I was her last hope. I was somewhat taken aback by the unannounced presence of this goddess-like Antipodean, to say the least. Eventually my brain functioned and slowly considered the odds of a stunning girl in a red bikini turning up at my tent on a dull, cold evening, somewhere in Herefordshire asking for chilli powder. I surreptitiously spied around in all directions expecting to discover the hidden camera of some reality television programme. My visitor having failed to receive a coherent answer after repeating herself several times, finally gave up and asked if I spoke English. Eventually I replied in the positive and handed over my jar of chilli powder. Having watched my visitor elegantly walk off to her pitch at the far end of the site, I turned around to find nearly the entire male population of the Tressek campsite doing the same.

I set about chopping up the ingredients for my stir-fry and soon had them frying away, when my chilli-hunting Aussie friend arrived again to return my spice. This time I was more coherent and discovered the Aussie pair were teachers from Perth working in London for two years. Of course, due to my concerns for this poor girl's health, I had to question the wearing of such a small bikini on such a cold day and discovered that the couple had been canoeing most of the day and she always wore a 'cossi' under her waterproof kit and due to getting the evening meal underway, hadn't got around to getting dressed yet. My visitor was also interested in my trip as she had noticed Mole and decided he was an odd craft to have on the Wye, but as my stir-fry was sticking to the pan through lack of attention, she thanked me for the chilli powder and disappeared again.

I finished my post-meal mug of coffee watching late arrivals in the adjacent site overflow field. Numerous passers-by on their way to the New Harp Inn or for an evening walk around Hoarwithy stopped for a word or two. Needless to say, the girl in the red bikini was a popular topic, at least for the men. I walked over to the river to check upon Mole and found him where he should have been. Even though it was dull and drab due to the dark, overcast clouds, the Wye had a quality, a charm or perhaps character. I realised I was missing my river and was now far happier in Mole on the river, than on land. That of course was how it should be. Being comfortable on the river confirmed my earlier misgivings about undertaking such a potentially dangerous trip with questionable health, to be unfounded.

Back at my nylon home, while tidying up my stuff I remembered to fill up my water container and finally dump the gathering rubbish I'd been transporting down the river for days. I made myself a mug of hot chocolate and retired for the evening. My mobile phone beeped away repeatedly when turned on, signifying everyone and their dog had sent a text message, so I spent a while confirming I was still alive and enjoying myself. That done, I turned my radio on and caught up with world events before drifting off to sleep.

My next day did not start well, as I was awakened far earlier than I had intended by some callow youth slapping the tent side and demanding camp fees. Having paid this individual, to my delight he asked if I wanted any firewood. I downed breakfast while watching the more energetic types who were now up and dragging or carrying canoes to make an early start on the river.

The nearby church of St. Catherine's was resplendent in the early morning sun, reminding me of my intentions to take a closer look. It made good sense to pack everything away before wandering off, so checking that my nylon neighbours were able to keep an eye upon my belongings, I packed away the tent and after making an orderly pile of my possessions, shouldered my rucksack and ambled my way towards Hoarwithy village. At the main road I turned right and eventually covered the few hundred yards to the church yard. For some unexplained reason, I hadn't realised that St. Catherine's was sat upon a knoll, which I found hard work to climb. After numerous stops to admire the view I summited the minor slope and arrived upon the threshold of my goal.

I had hoped to look inside the church, but a recent acquaintance from the campsite with the same intention, informed me that the doors were locked. Not surprisingly, a good number of other people were wandering around the church yard. Having ambled around the church exterior I entered the cloister or covered walkway which ran along the side of the church, to the campanile or bell tower. Here a couple of pews faced the open aspect of the cloister, providing those like me who needed to rest, a seat with a pleasant view through open archways supported upon smooth columns.

I liked St. Catherine's; whether its Byzantine-style befitted Herefordshire is another question, but I did admire the newly appointed vicar of 1854, who having decided that the original brick chapel lacked style, transformed the entire building at his own cost with local red sandstone, in the architectural style of Southern Italian Romanesque. It would be interesting to know what the congregation of the day thought about it all. I was eventually joined on my pew by a pair of ladies who had visited St. Catherine's some years earlier and assured me that I would find the design and craftsmanship on the inside was far more impressive than any external feature.

It seemed to take half the time to return to my pile of belongings, which after a short rest, I shuttled down to the river. A grey overcast sky replaced the earlier blue as I pulled Mole into the water and loaded up. Again the river and beach area was busy, but I was in no particular hurry and slowly manoeuvred my way out into the main stream towards my next camp some ten miles plus at Ross-on-Wye.

I had many curious canoeists for company and after two miles approached a rather nice pedestrian suspension bridge, which according to my guide, indicated I was nearing the village of Sellack. My map showed the village of Sellack to be on the right and Sellack Boat to be on the left, before Kings Caple. This delicate-looking bridge suspended by fine wire was built by Louis Harper of Aberdeen in 1895, to replace the long-established ford and ferry serving the villages of Sellack and Kings Caple. As if on cue, a group of Wye valley walkers crossed the bridge and paused to watch all pass beneath. Having exchanged pleasantries, I discovered the group to be en route to visit the nearby church of St. Tysilio, which in various constructions had served Sellack and parish since the seventh century.

I was quite taken with the idea of hiking through the magnificent countryside of the Wye valley and inspecting all the fine buildings and hostelries along the way, but that would probably have to be sometime in the future.

I was returned to the present by Mole banging and grinding through unseen shallows and for the hundredth time some obstacle lifted the left oar, which consequently lifted the left rowlock out of its fitting, thus rendering the oar useless. Normally this was just an annoying inconvenience, which required both hands to relocate the rowlock, but in fast rapids losing the ability to steer could be quite alarming.

A new set of nylon rowlocks had been purchased for the Wye adventure, with the original ones being stowed forward as spares. The new rowlocks were of smaller diameter, bought purposely to clasp the oar shaft and therefore making it harder to lose an oar. The rowlocks were themselves tied to the boat with a woven nylon line which ran through the centre of the rowlock fitting. My new rowlocks had shorter shafts and were designed to be retained in position by spring clips which fitted into groves around the bottom end of the shafts. Needless to say I forgot to obtain the clips, so every now and again, I suffered the inconvenience of having to replace the rowlock, but on a positive note, I never lost an oar.

As the river turned left I incurred a cool head wind which slowed progress considerably. A gaggle of red canoeists faring better against the wind than Mole began to catch up. After a brief exchange with the group leader I discovered this flotilla to be more youngsters undertaking the Duke of Edinburgh Award. As we neared the village of Strangford, landmarked by the two remaining stone pillars of yet another dismantled bridge of the Hereford to Gloucester railway I had been overhauled by the entire group apart from one straggler. One poor young chap who seemed pretty well done in, even with the repeated encouragement from his concerned instructor who shuttled back and forth like a mother blackbird delivering worms to an insatiable brood.

Still some ten yards away, the lad stopped paddling and slumped back in his seat. In answer to my concern the boy confirmed he was alright, but very tired with sore hands. A quick look over my shoulder affirmed his party to be a good distance away. I didn't want this young man to remember his Duke of Edinburgh Award experience to be a miserable affair, so decided to help him cheat. I rowed backwards towards him and threw the rope attached to Mole's transom and told him to hang on, while I gave him a tow, which he gratefully accepted.

I set up a respectable pace with the oars and like me the lad saw the funny side to our flouting of the rules. I kept a watchful eye out for the instructor and warned my passenger to drop the rope if and when his instructor came back. The twelfth-century Fawley Chapel was somewhere on the left, which according to my guide was "interesting" and also indicated that I had been towing my charge for one mile. From another glance over my shoulder, I noted the instructor coming towards us at a lick. I explained to my new young friend that we needed a good story in such circumstances. At the appropriate moment I indicated for the lad let go of the rope and continue to paddle right behind Mole.

As the instructor came alongside I explained that the poor young chap was suffering in the head wind, so I suggested he sheltered in the lee of Mole, which he found much easier. The instructor thanked me and asked whether I minded continuing in the same way until we arrived at their planned stop where the river turned back upon itself near How Caple, less than a mile further on. I replied that I would be pleased to do so and gave my new young friend a wink. The instructor turned about and sped off back to the main party. I waited awhile, then told my charge to pick up the rope and we set off again in tandem.

My tow was not much on conversation so I left him to his thoughts, while avoiding swans and keeping Mole going in a straight line in the blustering wind. Even though I was working hard, I started to feel the cold so added another layer. The instructor checked upon the wellbeing of my tow a couple of times more before we eventually neared the beach of small stones, adjacent to the village of How Caple, where the rest of the group were already setting about their sandwiches. My charge had released the rope and paddled up; he managed both a smile and a thank you, as did the concerned instructor as I passed.

"We can't help everyone, but everyone can help someone."

Dr. Loretta Scott

The headwind disappeared as the Wye began to loop back upon itself and I made more progress. My guide informed of 'salmon pools' for the next two miles and warned canoeists should keep to the bank indicated by green discs fixed to the trees and not red ones. I could see neither discs so nervously kept to the middle of the river until I eventually saw a tree with a green disc and moved nearer to the bank.

Over my right shoulder Lyndor Wood rose up steeply towards the farmed land at Perrystone, separated from the river by the old How Caple to Ross road. I decided it was time lunch and eventually came across a suitable spot to beach Mole and stretch my legs, albeit quite small.

The day had become brighter, if still mainly overcast, but without the wind it was quite warm. I walked up and down my new kingdom for a few minutes to get the blood flowing from my slightly enlarged ankles, while deciding what culinary delights I should prepare. I decided upon using up the last of my bacon with eggs, tomatoes and mushrooms. Once done I set my kettle to boil for my customary mug of tea.

Movement around the roots of a riverside tree caught my attention. Less than twenty feet away, a small black animal moved in and around the tree roots, as if looking or scenting for something and then it was gone. It had been too big to be a stoat or weasel and certainly the wrong colour. I've been a lifetime devotee of otters and it wasn't an otter. I discovered following research, that mink had been photographed on the Wye near Ross and the images certainly compared with the animal I saw, which was disappointing.

Again I found cooking and eating in the great outdoors very satisfying. I could understand why people made the life-changing decision to exchange city or suburban life for the wilderness. Whether I could become the complete hunter-gatherer is another matter. Now replete, I arranged my cargo to accommodate my usual siesta as the canoe group of my earlier encounter paddled by. My rather sad young friend was now being closely escorted by one of the instructors.

I opened my eyes some forty minutes or so later, to witness a major battle taking place overhead. A large raptor trying to soar upon the thermals was being harried by four black birds. Without my trusty WWII Canadian naval field-glasses it was hard to identify these masters of aerial combat. It was compelling to watch, high above the large bird of prey which I finally named as a buzzard, seemed to be content in just gliding around, but the black birds I decided were too large for rooks or crows and were perhaps ravens, would have none of it.

No doubt the buzzard was too close to a nest of young ravens and could probably have seen off a raven on a one-to-one basis, but not four to one. It was obviously that the ravens were acting as a well-coordinated team. If one raven harassed from the north and was about to receive retribution from the buzzard, then another raven came in from the south to distract the foe. Eventually the buzzard decided its intended prey wasn't worth the effort and slowly made off into the distance. This was always an enjoyable time; as I lay motionless I was able to observe all kinds of wildlife and especially the water fowl and swans up close as they paddled past Mole's stern.

With the show over my thoughts turned to coffee. Earlier in this tome I stated that I had left home with "everything but the kitchen sink". Some items were for use during the journey to the Wye, others were to be taken down the river or discarded to the boot of my car until my return. Somehow, the intended final selection process never happened and everything was piled into Mole. So it is with some embarrassment that I admit to be travelling the wild outdoors with a rather elegant cafetière coffee press, complete with ground coffee and brown sugar. Many books from my childhood told of cowboys on the plains or trappers along the Yukon, boiling coffee grains on campfires, but not one ever mentioned using a cafetière.

I decided a little self-indulgence wouldn't do any harm, so spooned a rather fine Columbian ground into the cafetière and poured on the boiling water. Having allowed for the appropriate brewing interval I lowered the filter press and poured a mug full of excellent coffee. Settling back once more I watched another family of ducks paddle by while enjoying my brew. While lost in my own little world, I hadn't noticed a couple of very proficient-looking chaps in a Canadian canoe approach. These two had it seemed, caught the smell of my coffee on the wind and found it incredulous that someone was actually brewing real coffee in the middle of nowhere. Needless to say, these two were willing recipients of my ground Colombian and were unanimous in declaring it to be the best coffee they had ever had.

With my new friends gone, I boiled another kettle of water and managed a barely palatable second press of coffee for my flask. Being once more ship shape and Bristol fashion I resumed my journey. My guide advised the next land mark to be "Hole-in-the-wall" and more rapids.

My arrival at the hamlet of "Hole-in-the-wall" was signified by a canoeing and outdoor centre on the left bank and a series of islands which served to both narrow and speed up the river. Surprisingly, Mole only scraped two boulders as he sped through the mildly exciting rapids. The bush-covered islands would have been a wild camper's dream. I didn't see a hole in a wall or any wall. The origins of "Hole-in-the-wall" are equally vague. Either the settlement took its name from an access point through some long-gone castle wall or a derivation of a pre-Norman term for 'hole-stone'.

Shortly I passed under the interesting suspended pedestrian bridge at Foy which enabled the congregation from the left bank of the Wye to worship at the nearby thirteenth-century St. Mary's church on the right bank. This, like many other Wye bridges had been repeatedly washed away. In its current form the bridge had stood since 1919. As I neared St. Mary's another bush-covered island divided the river but I passed through unscathed. I was fascinated by these little islands that must come and go at different times of the year with the changing water level. I regretted not landing on one of these mid-river islands, but so far I had not come across one at the time of my food or rest periods.

I had caught a brief glimpse of an unknown caravan site on the right bank, but now there was little to see. Farmed land rose gently up without feature on both sides of the bush- and tree-lined Wye. My constant companions the wildfowl were absent and had it seemed, decided to have the day off. The overcast sky and coolish weather made for a grey and dismal afternoon. For companionship I decided to listen to the spoken word on my little radio.

Next the river described a large 'S', with a tight turn to the right followed by an equally tight turn to the left. This meander created a selection of nice stone beaches, weedy shallows, minor rapids and of course, was complete with the mandatory remains of stone bridge pillars from my other constant companion, the ghost of the defunct Hereford to Gloucester railway. This according to my guide was Backney Common, my next landmark, where on the left bank is a simple metal cross commemorating an act of bravery in 1904 by Reverend Helier Evans, the rector of nearby Brampton Abbotts, who died whilst saving his son and daughter's friend from drowning. Try as I could, I could not spot this monument.

From here my overnight stop was three miles away at Willton just after Ross-on-Wye. I made good progress along this straight part of the river, with assistance from a slight breeze. My map indicated Ashe Ingen Court, a sizable house with medieval origins to be on the right, but riverside trees prevented the merest peek. Following gentle left and right turns, the Wye straightens out to provide views of the modern A40 road bridge and the town of Ross beyond. Once under the A40 I shipped the oars and drifted while sampling the contents of my flask and a sizable lump of flapjack. My presence was again of considerable interest to the practiced oarsmen and oarswomen setting out from the Ross-on-Wye Rowing Club on the left bank. Having someone drinking coffee from a mug and eating cake while sat in a small dinghy was certainly incongruous to these fine athletes, so having answered the usual questions I moved on without my ritual of bestowing gifts of cake upon the natives.

At Ross the Wye adopts a traditional horseshoe shape, with a surprising number of swans, and is overseen by the towering 200-foot spire of St. Mary's Church. Patrons of the riverside beer garden undaunted by the dull weather enjoyed their early evening revelry and waved as I sculled by. Having completed the Wye horseshoe I neared the village of Wilton, briefly catching sight of the ruined Wilton castle set back on the right. This twelfth-century Norman castle was mainly destroyed during the Civil War to prevent it being garrisoned. Interestingly the castle is receiving restoration works and is inhabited by the current owner.

Finally, I was rewarded with the welcomed sight of the late sixteenth-century Wilton road bridge, which carried the now busy B4260. Originally the six-arch red sandstone bridge transported the toll road connecting Gloucester and Hereford and like the bridge at Hereford, temporarily lost an arch due to Civil War defensive measures. In common with all Wye bridges, Wilton had taken a battering from river forces and had to have its pillars reinforced in 1914. This Grade 1 listed bridge gained an odd sort of pedestal-mounted, spherical sundial in the early eighteenth century, which I spotted once as I passed under and decided was worthy of closer inspection. After the bridge the Wye picked up the pace and some fifty-odd yards on the right bank stood the White Lion Inn, my destination for the evening.

With some effort I pulled across the current and made for a jetty formed from a dozen or so large stones, extending outward into the river. Without the protection of this little harbour landing would have be very difficult. Between the inn and the river was a nicely mown strip of grass, upon which stood a few small tents, all lined up against the pub garden's retaining wall. With Mole secured to a big stone I took in my surroundings. The river was without doubt, closer to my tent pitch than any of my previous campsites, but how to clamber up the eight feet of steep, slippy, red earth to get there was another problem.

Somewhat precariously, I scrambled up the minor cliff on all fours to the camping grass and wandered into the White Lion in search of someone to report my arrival. While awaiting the appropriate person, I was encouraged to note the dining area was doing good trade and so possibly worthy of my patronage. My induction to camping at the White Lion began with a tour of the adequate ablution facility, housed in a sort of draughty annex and a reminder that to have a shower would require the correct coinage. Back outside again, the innkeep explained the necessity for pitching my tent as close to the inn's retaining wall as possible, due to this bit of grass being a public right of way.

It would seem that the local authority was not at all happy about this patch of green being used as a campsite. This situation, the White Lion claimed very apologetically, required the issuing of an eight-point memorandum to all prospective campers. In reality, only two points concerned the forbidding of large tents, cooking and the use of bottles and glasses on the riverbank; the remaining six points were specific to the White Lion's own rules and regulations. I found item three interesting, as it explained that campers were offered, providing the order was placed before 9pm on the previous evening, a full English breakfast complete with all the trimmings at an almost reasonable rate, but claimed not to have the "facilities to provide cereals etc." I wasted a disproportionate amount of time pondering what kind of different or extra facilities would be need to throw a few cornflakes into a bowl? I admit with some embarrassment, that it was some time before I realised that it wasn't a question of facilities, it was simply a matter of profitability or rather lack of it.

Rather gingerly I descended the minor escarpment down to Mole, trying carefully not to break into a quick trot and end up full length in the river. I had just made the relative safety of the pier of large stones, when a mad, bear-sized golden retriever hurtled down the riverbank and leapt past me into the river, where it continued to bound around excitedly waist deep in the water. After three or four attempts, the innkeep finally managed to persuade the mad beast to return, if not somewhat reluctantly, to the inn. This playful dog I would learn was very popular with both campers and inn patrons alike, especially as it would at every opportunity, escape from the bar to end up bounding around in the river, barking excitedly.

While I was trying to work out the best method for transporting my boxes and stuff up this slippy cliff, a couple of chaps in a canoe arrived and after much slipping and cursing managed to get their canoe up onto the bank. After a certain amount of trial and error and a good deal of swearing and cursing by myself, I discovered I could just place a box at the top of this minor cliff, where the grassed slope began. However, my plastic boxes refused to stay put on the grass and slid over the edge, down the steep bank, to then scatter their contents into the river. I discovered that the waterproof bags containing my tent, sleeping bag and air bed etc. would stay put and so, I constructed a retaining barrier of these bags along the grass edge and then placed the boxes behind them. With all Mole's cargo perilously positioned along the mini cliff edge, I scrambled up and set about shuttling everything over to my pitch up against the inn's retaining wall.

Setting up camp took a little longer than normal due to numerous chats and conversations undertaken with my fellow river-travelling campers. Having ensured the appropriate assortment of coins, I sorted a change of clothes and ablution kit, and then set off to take advantage of the showers before dining at the inn. A canoeing family of my earlier encounter had just eaten at the White Lion and spoke enthusiastically about their helping of liver and bacon. Needless to say, even a shower in the chilly outbuilding couldn't stop me thinking exclusively of liver and bacon, which made me feel extremely hungry.

The White Lion's bar/restaurant was reasonably appointed in traditional manner and offered a convivial ambience. I ordered my much anticipated meal, a bottle of local cider and found myself an empty table. I passed the time by entering the day's events into my journal until my meal arrived. After a reasonable interval, the venerated fare arrived, of which both quality and quantity satisfied my expectations. While finishing off with coffee, I swapped anecdotes with another group of Wye travellers sitting at the next table.

I had enjoyed dinning at the White Lion, but even though the 'no cooking' by-law had mitigated the event, I still felt a little uneasy about breaking my 'total self-catering' undertaking. This uneasiness turned into extreme self-annoyance the next morning when I discovered that the White Lion had provided a designated 'cooking area' adjacent to the camping area, which I had somehow overlooked, as it was clearly stated in the Lion's "Regulations".

I was now starting to feel rather drowsy and although relatively early, considered it about time to head back to my sleeping bag. Once outside I took advantage of the inn's external lights to check my mobile phone. The usual text requests for progress reports had piled in along with a missed call from home.

Suspecting some problematic issue I returned the call, but it was only my wife Viv calling for a chat. Remembering the White Lion had one of the two webcams along the Wye, I suggested to fire up my laptop and then she would be able to see Mole at his moorings. Viv could just about make out Mole in the gloom, so for some unexplained reason I climbed on top of a garden table and started waving at the webcam mounted under the eaves of the inn. Forgetting that the webcam's image took some time to refresh, I was a source of consternation for numerous passers-by, as I stood on the table top in the half light, waving like an idiot at the inn's roof and shouting, "Can you see me now?"

CHAPTER 9

Oh, what a beautiful morning!

Esteem they precious time,
Which pass so swift away
Prepare thee for eternity
And do not make delay.

Anon,
Inscribed around the sundial on Wilton Bridge.

I awoke to an absolutely magnificent morning of bright sunshine, blue sky and a river full of pristine white swans. I had the tent down and everything packed away on Mole in record time; I couldn't wait to get out on the river and experience the next eight miles to my next camp. After a quick visit to the White Lion's wash facilities I was away. Once out into the main stream the current pushed Mole along at a good rate. Here the river became wider, reflecting the blue sky apart from where the big cotton wool clouds and tall riverbank trees cast dark shadows. Unsure whether it was due to the bright sunshine, but the increased number of willows along the bank seemed to provide a brighter, more pleasant or softer edge to the Wye.

The hundreds of unpaired swans let me pass without incident. Looking at Wilton Bridge now a hundred yards or so back, I could just make out the unique sundial standing proud above the parapet, reminiscent of a lone sentry. It was such a pleasurable morning and as I wasn't in any hurry, I decided to ship the oars and just drift, while I leant back and enjoyed the view.

> *"Be happy for this moment. This moment is your life."*
> Omar Khayyam

Beyond the tree-lined banks, agricultural land gently rolled away. On the left, the land slowly rose some six hundred feet to the wooded mound of Chase Hill, the onetime site of an Iron Age fort and Roman settlement. I heard from local sources that the Wye was surprisingly deep around Ross, with currents and strong undertows that had claimed many lives over the years. I could believe the water below Mole was rather deep, but it looked more inviting than intimidating, so it was to a degree, perhaps understandable why swimmers got into trouble.

I'd forgone the option of using the White Lion's "designated cooking area" for preparing my breakfast, in favour of getting out on the river sooner, and elected to eat somewhere along the way, sometime later. Mole had drifted quite happily for a while and had only needed the odd course correction. I was now seriously ready for breakfast and according to my map, the river was about to undertake a couple of considerable meanders, so it was probably the best time to tie up to a riverside bush and get the kettle going afloat.

Porridge, tinned apricots and coffee had never tasted better! I'd just adopted my repose position with coffee in hand, when a flash of metallic blue entered my line of vision on the opposite bank. A kingfisher had landed upon a branch of a riverside bush, allowing clear sight of his blue and orange plumage. Then having seemingly checked the coast to be clear, it disappeared somewhere into the riverbank, with the precise location obscured by pile of driftwood left high and dry by the last flood tide. Within a few seconds the bird appeared again and set off upstream following the shallows. After a few minutes the kingfisher returned to its perch and then flew off back upstream again. I couldn't tell how successful my little friend was at fishing, for although he or she repeatedly flew back and forth, I never saw a beak full of fish.

With renewed vigour, I took up the oars and set a good rate. I navigated the two meanders without fuss, apart from the odd scrape or two passing through shallows where the Wye neared the A40. From my map, I knew somewhere on the left I was passing the rather impressive Grade II listed building Homme House, with origins dating back to the early sixteenth century and set in an estate of some one hundred acres of parkland, landscaped by the omnipresent Lancelot 'Capability' Brown. The ruins of a fourteenth-century castle, once belonging to the original estate owners can still be seen. Apparently the endeavours of Homme House during WWII as a military hospital were acknowledged by both the Red Cross and Her Majesty the Queen.

I also passed somewhere on the right, the Georgian Grade II listed Glewstone Court, which like many of the fine houses along the Wye, had become a hotel specialising in wedding receptions. I could easily imagine the gentry from times past, strolling pensively along the river, being masters of all they surveyed. However, I was soon brought back to the present by the sight of fields full of poly tunnels. I suppose if I should consider hectares of polythene to be incompatible with the beauty of the Wye valley, then the numerous diesel-engined irrigation pumps drawing water from the Wye, which banged away day and night, were certainly incongruous with the natural serenity. However, I do have sympathy with folk who have to earn a living in areas of great natural beauty, always having their actions scrutinised by the rest of us who insist that their workplace is maintained picture perfect for our leisure purposes.

Eventually I caught my first glimpse of Goodrich Castle, standing proud above the trees. I remembered reading that some of the most esteemed eighteenth-century poets and artists beat a path to Goodrich to experience the stunning views. Having visited these parts some years earlier, I knew there would be a better view of this majestic eleventh-century castle further on. On the left the land rose up to the magnificent Howle Hill and the medieval earthworks of Great Howle beyond. I was always uplifted by a good panorama, whereas stretches of the river absent of wildlife and with little to see, due to tunnel-like bushes and trees, were mildly depressing. Usually, this melancholia had to be remedied by self-administering regular fruitcake or flapjack.

Lost in my surroundings, I was soon approaching the very solid stone construction that is Kerne Bridge, built in 1828 to facilitate passage from Walford to Goodrich on the B4229. I quite liked the symmetry of the bridge's five arches, reducing equally in size from the middle outwards. The significance of this bridge to the locality must have been considerable, as following its construction the adjacent hamlet of 'The Quern', became known as Kerne Bridge.

On the right-hand bank just before the bridge stands the rather splendid Flanesford Priory. The original building gained a mention in the Doomsday Book, with the priory being founded later in 1346 by Sir Richard Talbot, Lord of Goodrich Castle. Habitation by the order of Augustinian monks ceased in 1537 with the Dissolution of Monasteries. It seems that following Dissolution, George Talbot the 3rd Earl of Shrewsbury was granted title to the priory for a pittance. With the end of the Talbot lineage in 1616, the fine priory was eventually used as farm buildings up until 1980, when suffering the final indignity of conversion into holiday homes.

Unlike all the bridges encountered so far, the Wye flowed through the arches of Kerne Bridge in the most placid manner. Immediately through the bridge, the river formed a pleasant pool complete with beach, due to the once mid-river large island all but joining up with the left-hand bank. This being an ideal spot, I declared it time for lunch and drove Mole ashore. I did my usual brief exploration of my new kingdom whilst enjoying the midday sun. On the left bank I could just see the roof of the 'Inn on the Wye' above the tall grass and bushes, which along with the B4324 was nearer to the river than I remembered.

In the interest of expediency, I declared lunch to be curried baked beans and sausage with instant noodles. Once prepared, I laid out my food and tea upon Mole's foredeck, positioned my 'director's chair' appropriately and began luncheon in a very civil manner. Two forkfuls in, I was hailed by my first canoeists of the day, who insisted I should enter into a major debate upon the merits of Wye travel. Finishing of the now cold beans and noodles, I fancied rounding off my feast with peanut butter and raspberry jam. Fishing around in Mole's right buoyancy compartment I found the rather elderly French loaf. The French loaf was chosen as reserve ration, due to its profile which enabled passage through the buoyancy compartment access hole.

The layers of plastic bags and aluminium foil had maintained the bread in reasonable condition, as in stale but not mouldy. It was edible but not enjoyable, but toasted on my gas stove it was marvellous and proved the perfect base for peanut butter and jam. I was joined briefly by a group of Wye valley walkers who had crossed over Kerne Bridge to lunch at the inn behind me.

It occurred that my little crescent-shaped beach would make for an ideal photo opportunity. I retrieved my tripod from Mole's left buoyancy compartment and set it up at the other end of my beach, with camera attached. Originally I had thought I would row with my camera and tripod set up in Mole's stern so I could quickly and easily take photos as I went along, which turned out to be totally impractical. My planned intention was to take a photo of myself sat down next to Mole, using the camera's delayed shutter function. Having focussed upon Mole I set the delay timer for ten seconds, pressed the shutter and walked back to Mole. Just before I got to Mole I heard the camera shutter click. Fortunately being a digital camera I could check the picture and found a reasonable shot of Mole, but I was nowhere to be seen. I reset the camera and pressed the shutter and this time, I half jogged the ten yards back to Mole but to no avail, as I heard the shutter click whilst just in the action of sitting down. The next time I set the delay for twenty seconds, and pressed the shutter. I hurried back to Mole as fast as I could, sat down and struck up a suitable pose. Believing that the twenty-second delay period must had lapsed I stood up, only to hear the confounded click of the shutter.

Not only was I quickly losing patience with this project I was also shattered, but decided to give it just one more go. I rechecked the camera with great care and in a flash of inspiration, realised I could monitor the lapsed time with my watch. So I synchronised the twenty-second delay with my watch, strode back to Mole and struck up a pose while all the time monitoring the delay time on my watch. The second hand of my timepiece was approaching twenty seconds, when a pair of black Labradors bounded out of the bushes behind me and leaped straight into the river. Needless to say, I now had a perfect action shot of 'Labradors in flight', but with me totally obscured.

The dog owner put in a brief appearance and having rendered the mad hounds under control, disappeared again. I was now very weary with all the 'toing and froing' and starting to believe the world was conspiring against me. However, I was determined to achieve this photographic study of 'man with boat' if it killed me. Firstly I headed up the short track towards the road and scanned the horizon for further potential interruptions, then it was back to the camera which was set and synchronised with my watch. After setting the shutter I made it back to Mole in good time, but for some unexplained reason, I stuck my bush hat on my head and took up my mug of cold tea. Nevertheless, I do have a perfect picture of an old idiot sat by a boat, wearing an odd hat and holding a mug. In laboured fashion, I collected up and stowed the photographic equipment, then fashioned a suitable pillow from my folded air bed and settled down aboard Mole for my afternoon siesta.

At some undeterminable time later, I regained consciousness to witness a strange 'Lady of the Lake' vision. Just a few yards away, in the middle of the river, sat a young girl with great mane of golden hair, which dazzled in the bright sunlight. Not believing my own eyes, I raised myself up onto an elbow, and only then with a better view did I realise that the young lady was not performing a miracle or holding Excalibur, but was actually kneeling upon a surfboard holding a paddle.

Without thinking in my semi-conscious state, I questioned the young lady upon her journey's origin, to which she replied some unintelligible location while seeming preoccupied by someone or something upriver beyond Kerne Bridge. Next, two canoes appeared from under the bridge and after a short dialogue with the occupants, the young girl stood up and propelled herself off downstream with a long paddle.

Initially, I had to admire the competence and confidence of this girl to take on the Wye on a surfboard, but in hindsight I think she was perhaps foolhardy in not wearing safety gear. When recounting this tale later in the day, I learnt that the young lady's craft was indeed a 'paddleboard' and not a surfboard.

I readied Mole for our afternoon stint and when done, spent a moment or two treating the abundant tiny fish that darted around the shallows, to breadcrumbs left over from my toast production. With the mini feeding frenzy over, I climbed aboard Mole and pushed out into the river and after a few strokes was quickly taken by the increasing current, caused by my island narrowing the river. Keeping to the right-hand bank I navigated the shallows and narrows created by two further mid-river islands as the Wye turned to the left. It really was a perfect day, the kind I had hoped to experience every day. The sun had been ever present and I realised that my arms and knees were starting to burn. I had of course forgotten to the all-important sunscreen, so having shipped the oars I rooted out the appropriate balm and applied it to all my exposed skin. I made a note to self; remember the application of sun cream each morning before setting off. I really didn't need to succumb to sunburn as well as swollen ankles and an ever increasingly painful rear end.

Whilst pausing to enjoy my surroundings before taking up the oars, I noted some erratic movement around the trunk of a near riverside tree. Although of considerable girth, the tree had sometime previously lost its upper trunk and branches, possible evidence of a lightning strike. Scurrying around the remaining ivy-covered trunk at great pace, were numerous mouse-like creatures, being dark brown in colour with light underbellies. It took a few moments to remember these creatures were actually birds of the 'Treecreeper' variety. I'd been bemused when first encountering the antics of these fascinating birds some twenty-five years earlier, when on a family camping trip to Betws-y-Coed in North Wales. We had stood mesmerised watching dozens of these small birds frantically charge around an ivy-covered tree on the banks of the River Llugwy.

Leaving the frenzied birds behind, the Wye began a slow bend to the right, in readiness for the start of the tight loop somewhere ahead. Sadly traffic noise from the B4234 that had accompanied the Wye through the valley became more noticeable, although out of view. Beyond the left-hand bank rose up the hump-shaped Coal Hill, with steep-sided wooded valleys carved around each side, which now guide small brooks into the Wye. At the foot of Coal Hill stands the more homely than stately Bishopswood House, built in 1844. Of more interest than the house is the surrounding land. This once 2,000-acre estate, which had seen Roman presence, was also in Norman times classified for the purpose of hunting, an activity that continued through the fifteenth century by the successive Bishops of Hereford. From the current owner's promotional material we learn that King Henry V, he of Agincourt fame, was rumoured to have hunted the estate, but claims that Wellington however, the Iron

Duke, certainly did.

High on the right with a commanding view over the Wye loop stands the fascinating Courtfield manor house. Although originally named Greyfield or Greenfield, the manor changed its name after Henry V took up residence when aged eight, following the death of his mother in 1395. Given that Henry was born only a few miles away at Monmouth and then lived at Courtfield, his rumoured hunting at Bishopswood a few yards across the river seems quite probable. I found it rather moving to think I was in the middle of the great Henry's childhood playground and suddenly felt compelled to raise an arm skyward and shout, "Cry God for Harry, England and Saint George!" Then having rather sheepishly checked the nearby riverbanks for any witnesses to my proclamation, I rowed on.

For the future incumbents at Courtfield life proved to be far from idyllic. In 1562 the Vaughan family took up residence, but due to their continued devotion to Roman Catholicism, suffered persecution, fines, confiscation of lands and imprisonment. The family would lose more than half of their ancestral land in confiscation and in 1651, the Courtfield manor house was sequestered, with goods and livestock being auctioned off. Further members of the family fought alongside the Jacobites at Culloden and had to flee to Spain following the defeat of Charles Stuart's army. For this escapade, the pair suffered exclusion from George II's pardon of 1747 and additional property seizure. With passage of the nineteenth century and many marriages and inheritances, the family's fortunes were restored along with that of Courtfield. In 1950 the Courtfield house and some estate land was sold to the Mill Hill Missionary Society, originally founded by Vaughan family member, Cardinal Herbert Vaughan. Courtfield was sold again in 2004.

Approaching the top of the Wye's loop, the three sprawling hamlets of Lydbrook came into view. The trio of Lower, Central and Upper Lydbrook rise up from river level and mark the north-west edge of the Forest of Dean's Gloucestershire boundary. Like many Wye villages, Lydbrook had seen Roman habitation and widespread finds of flint tools indicates extensive occupation and farming for 4,000 years or more. It was difficult to associate this now peaceful panorama with heavy industries of previous times. For centuries the locality had seen considerable mining of coals and iron ore, along with iron working and tin plate production. In the early twentieth century, Lydbrook became a renowned producer of electrical cable.

From that much revered grandmaster of Wye observation William Gilpin, we learn that in 1770 Lydbrook was *"served by a large wharf, from where barges of coals set forth for Hereford and the like"*. Gilpin after surveying all the hustle and bustle of loading and unloading of barges against the scenic backdrop of wooded hills, declared *"the variety of view did together produce a picturesque assemblage"*.

The eighteenth-century Courtfield Arms appeared on the left, just a stone's throw from the river across the B4324, and would have made for a good stop, confirmed by the number of parked canoes. My preoccupation with the inn caused me to almost run aground upon a mid-river island and after some panic evasive action followed by a lot crunching and scraping I resumed my course.

Almost imperceptibly the current had increased to a surprisingly fast rate and I now became a little anxious about being shot past my next overnight stop at the YHA campsite at Welsh Bicknor on the right bank, as opposed to English Bicknor on the left. Here once again the Welsh-English border ran down the middle of the river. From my notes, I knew I had to look out for a YHA sign and a stone landing, so to enable me to spot the landing stage in good time, I reduced Mole's speed by reverse rowing. Eventually a gap in the riverside skyline foliage appeared, which turned out to be the position of a rather good stone landing and after a great deal of effort I managed to row across the fast flow and reach my safe haven.

I was immediately impressed by my new overnight stop, as the differential between river and land was only a few yards up a gentle slope. The landing was constructed in the usual design to cope with the ever changing water level, having a series of four stone steps which ran along the river's edge for around fifteen feet. At one end just above river level, a stone jetty of some twelve feet extended out into the water, which made for an ideal mooring. While looking around for a suitable bush or tree upon which to tie Mole, I was immediately joined by fourteen ducks, which had appeared from nowhere and now ran up and down the jetty as if looking for a suitable spot to jump aboard Mole. This unruly but mesmerising mob seemed to be of two adults with broods of differing ages, one juvenile and the other very young chicks. Although it was very entertaining to be in such close proximity to these mad waterfowl, I was a little perplexed as to how I could unload Mole in the middle of such mayhem.

Gathering up Mole's painter I clambered onto the jetty on all fours; my new feathered friends didn't seemed bothered, rather than taking flight they just moved out of the way and carried on with their preoccupation. So having waded cautiously through the throng of ducks I rather stiffly made it up the approach to the camping site. I was immediately captivated by a vast expanse of green vitality. In front of me a little more than a hundred yards to the north, a wooded escarpment of dark green foliage formed a curtain wall from east to west, which contrasted against acres of recently mown bright green grass extending without occupation both east and west. Again I was treated to that special low, late afternoon sun which not only gave everything a golden hue but also heightened definition. Of course the bright blue sky with clouds like giant lumps of brilliant white cotton wool contributed to the whole magnificent panorama. If ever there was a scene that was decidedly 'picturesque' it was here and now, so having hitched Mole's painter to a handy sapling, I retrieved my camera and captured the stunning piece of nature for posterity, as they say.

For a while I just stood and enjoyed the tranquillity, the warming sun and the soft breeze that turned the leaves of the riverside trees to reveal their lighter shade. My exclusivity of the campsite was short-lived as I spied in the distance a campervan slowly approaching from the west. Eventually my new neighbours arrived and passed with the usual nod of acknowledgement. With the mood broken I returned to battle with the insane ducks and shuttled Mole's cargo up to the site. I'd dumped all my stuff at the top of the landing access point, near to the position of the site water tap. It was to this tap that my new neighbour now was heading with plastic water carrier. I'd noted my cohabiter had set up home a good eight or ten feet in from the edge of the campsite or where the mowing had ended, leaving a substantial margin of long grass, cow parsley and rosebay willowherb between the riverbank trees and bushes.

After a few minutes of exchanging anecdotes upon camping and the like, my new water-carrying friend enquired whether he could assist in the transportation of my great pile of possessions. Having declined the kind offer, I explained that I would probably pitch where I was, as close proximity to the river access would minimise the amount of lugging stuff and also allow relatively easy surveillance of Mole. As my new water-carrying friend was an experienced user of the site, he advised to pitch my tent a few paces in from the edge, explaining that The Wye Valley Way footpath followed the river through our campsite and if campers didn't line up their accommodations to form a distinct passageway, endless groups of walkers rambled lost around the tents, falling over guy ropes and the like. Being the first and last tent of this Wye super highway, I was during my short stay, required to act as guide on more than one occasion.

Sufficiently rested, I set about sorting the tent and when done, sat for a while just enjoying my new surroundings. Having refreshed my spiritual inner self, I resisted the urge to hug a tree and thought it appropriate to announce my arrival to the YHA and pay my camp fees, so set off in search of the site office. My slow amble eventually brought me to a stand of trees extending out into the campsite which had to my surprise, totally obscured the quaint little Church of St. Margaret. My later reading upon St. Margaret's suggested the original church dated from the fourteenth century, but the present incarnation was the result of significant rebuilding carried out in 1858. I was also interested to learn that the little church had been the home of a recumbent female effigy believed to date from the late thirteenth or early fourteenth century.

From this position, I could now see the substantial two-storey YHA hostel, which had previously served as the rectory to the little church. This was another interesting building with sixteenth-century origins and seventeenth-century additions. Upon arriving at the hostel, I discovered the reception to be closed, but a little notice informed that it would reopen in half an hour, so decided to avail myself of the facilities. Relieved and washed I undertook a minor tour of the hostelry and from my brief observations, it was obviously a popular and ideal place to stay. I sat outside for a while, chatting and exchanging pleasantries with numerous hostellers until the reception's opening time arrived.

A small queue had formed at reception, allowing time to read all the lost and found notices and site by-laws displayed on the adjacent wall. My turn at the window eventually arrived where a pleasant young gentleman processed my camping fee payment in a pleasant manner. During this brief exchange my eyes fixed upon a surprisingly good menu offered by the hostel, along with an even more surprising good wine list. This was a far cry from my austere hostelling experience of the 1960s and I couldn't resist purchasing a couple of bottles of rather fine local cider.

I returned to my tent at a slow saunter, pausing for a recuperative rest at the little church. A small convoy of two Land Rover Discoveries with roof-mounted Canadian canoes and troops of small children wallowed slowly by. By the time I reached my tent the new canoeing neighbours had set about erecting their nylon accommodation. This lot were obviously serious campers, as in addition to tents, a sizable covered cooking and eating area was assembled adjacent to the two larger tents. It was time for food so I prepared a rather tasty bacon luncheon meat pasta carbonara. I positioned my folding chair to allow maximum observation of the magnificent Wye landscape and set about consuming my superb pasta which I washed down with an even more superb cider. This really was a special time.

Hail! land of cyder, vales of health!
Redundant fruitage, rural wealth;
Here, did Pomona still retain,
Her influence o'er a British plain,
Robert Bloomfield

Replete and in reflective mood, I considered my good fortune. My newest neighbour passed by my threshold with water carrier and upon his return from the tap stopped for a chat. I learnt that this rather affable young fellow, Dominic, was a regular canoeist of the Wye and along with wife and young children would be taking to the river in the morning. After many chats, Dominic and I discovered we shared many interests which included undertaking precarious adventures, and have remained in regular contact since. However,

Dominic and lovely wife Nicola's adventuring far surpassed my exploits, when in 2004 they undertook a 2,300-mile, life-threatening circumnavigation of the British Isles in a twenty-foot Hardy Pilot motor cruiser. This was obviously a trip of a lifetime, but to their credit Dominic and Nicola used the event to raise considerable funds for the Motor Neurone Disease Association.

It was a stunning evening and deserving of celebrative good coffee, so I ambled down to the river to retrieve my cafetière from Mole's innards. Nearing the landing I was treated to the most amusing sight. The mad ducks were back and the whole group were in unison practising 'ducking and diving' in the safety of the eddy provided by the jetty. It was the funniest thing; the two mother ducks would up-end, immediately followed by the entire brood of fourteen doing the same. I sat and watched this hilarious spectacle of upside-down ducks for a while, before eventually grabbing the cafetière.

I had just given the duck ensemble one last look and was returning up the bank, when my attention was attracted by shouts from the river. I turned to see two men and a boy of around twelve years standing upon what I initially thought to be three squares of wood mid-river. The leading man held a coil of rope which he desperately wanted me to catch and tie on to something, before the anxious trio were swept away downriver. Having caught the rope and assured that Mole was securely moored, I tied the rope onto Mole's stern and then with some effort began pulling the trio towards the jetty. With the threesome padding like fury and me pulling, the strange craft eventually made it to safety.

Once on dry land, my three new grateful friends explained their plight. The father and his brother were trialling a prototype raft to be used in future Wye raft races. His idea was to construct a raft on a modular basis, so that one could simply add another module to accommodate each additional paddler. The module design consisted of two large watertight plastic pipes held in parallel position with quick-form aluminium scaffolding tubes, with a plywood walkway board on top. The three modules had been held together in a line by flexible joints. I had to applaud the design, far better than the ridged oil drum or large war canoe models I had witnessed struggle through the shallows and rapids a few days before and of course, I was impressed with the module design.

However, like all designs, the 'devil is in the detail'. Apparently the raft had worked successfully and coped with a range of rapids and shallows until the large plastic pipes began to fill with water. I could see the holes in the plastic pipes used for fixing the scaffolding tubes had been drilled far too big for the fixing bolt diameters, easily allowing the ingress of water. Initially all would have been fine, until waves and splashes reached the top of the plastic pipes. Then with the inflow of water the pipes would sit lower in the river, making it easier for further water to enter through the bolt holes. So by the time the raft reached my jetty, the pipes were virtually full of water and about to plunge to the depths. This is why I could at first, only see the plywood seating as the supporting pipes were all but submerged.

The group were certainly shaken and obviously grateful for my intervention, if not a little embarrassed. Although I supported the quest, I was more than a little perturbed by the lack of life jackets! There was a slightly humorous aspect to this escapade, as the designer had arranged for his wife to meet him along the Wye, in order to transport crew and raft back home. The arrangement being that both parties would set off down the Wye simultaneously, one by river, the other by road. When the rafting party had completed satisfactory trials and found a suitable landing site, the designer would inform his wife by mobile phone of their location and subsequent collection. However, the raft had ploughed on downriver, missing one after another the previously designated landing sites. Each time the very anxious wife stood on the riverbank awaiting the expected raft, it raced past with her husband shouting instructions to hurry on to the next landing. Once ashore the raft designer was able to assure his now concerned wife that all was well and provide directions to their final location.

The raft had to be removed quickly from the water before it disappeared forever. So one by one we managed to drag the exceedingly heavy modules onto the landing. The water-filled rafts were far too heavy to move further and could not be easily drained, so the only option was to stand the pipes upright thus allowing the water to drain out through the bolt holes by which it came in. To any passing river craft, this strange collection of vertical grey plastic pipes would seem to have no practical purpose and was perhaps some modern riverside sculpture.

Rather weary, I staggered up the riverbank back to my tent and set my little kettle to boil. I quickly made a cup of instant coffee and having sliced through the securing tape on my second tin of flapjack, selected myself a largish lump. I returned once more to just sitting and enjoying the panorama, when suddenly remembered that I'd left my cafetière down by the river, so it was back down the bank to restore the coffee maker to its hiding place within Mole. My day was made complete when my mad duck friends started returning to the landing. I discovered that I still had a half-eaten piece of flapjack in my pocket, where it had been temporarily stored while messing with the cafetière, so having reduced it to crumbs, I scattered it around among the milling throng.

The majority of these crazy fowl were not at all interested in my flapjack crumbs and just ran around wildly, so I presumed they hadn't yet developed a taste for human handouts. Equally perplexing was the fact that none of these wild creatures demonstrated a fear of human beings. According to the YHA staff, it was still early in the season for river campers, so the ducks hadn't had much exposure to humans in their short lives. I could only assume, that it was because they hadn't yet encountered the cruelty and stupidity of humans, that they were still fearless.

Back at the tent I decided upon another cup of coffee while bringing my journal up to date. It had been both an enjoyable and eventful day. I really liked the campsite and although the major hike to the amenities was a bit irksome, the location was just perfect. It only occurred to me some weeks later, that I could have stayed an additional day or more at Welsh Bicknor or anywhere that took my fancy, as I wasn't in a hurry and didn't have to adhere to a strict schedule and after all, it was all about the journey rather than arriving at the destination.

CHAPTER 10

Sad Farewell to Ducks!

My soul is an enchanted boat,
Which, like a sleeping swan, doth float.
Percy Bysshe Shelly

I must have slept fitfully, as I awoke much later than normal or had intended. Gathering up my wash gear, I began the long trek to the YHA hostel and had just returned as my new friend Dominic and extended family set off downriver. It was a pleasant morning and my few neighbours had all been up and gone by the time I was setting about my breakfast. Breakfasting alfresco in the warm morning sun, surrounded by such natural beauty, was very therapeutic. Such was this soporific effect, that I almost nodded off. I was suddenly brought awake and back to reality with the realisation that I had ahead of me, my second longest daily journey of twelve miles to my next camp at Monmouth. I was at least two hours behind schedule and needed to get stowed away and off downriver as soon as possible.

Being less than meticulous about my packing, I soon had everything ready for transportation down the riverbank to Mole. I had hoped the sections of modular raft from the previous evening's debacle would have been retrieved from the jetty before I had to load Mole, but no such luck. Nearing the strange tubes, I placed my boxes on the landing and tested the weight of the upright pair of floatation cylinders blocking my access to Mole. The tubes moved easily, indicating that the tens of gallons of Wye water had drained away overnight. I checked the other two pairs and found them to be the same, so I move all three raft modules to the far end of the landing, which now allowed an unobstructed passage to Mole.

Having lugged all my belongings down into Mole and satisfied that I hadn't left any vital piece of equipment behind, I untied Mole's mooring and climbed aboard. From out of nowhere, the mad ducks arrived on the jetty and started their frantic ritual. One of the elder brood jumped aboard Mole and was suddenly joined by numerous siblings. This was of course highly amusing, but last thing I needed was a boat full of ducks when trying to make a quick getaway. Unsurprisingly, members of the younger brood also wanted to emulate their elder cousins and were tentatively exploring the possibilities of jumping aboard. Serious measures were called for.

Herding ducks is like herding sheep. In trying to encourage them one way out of Mole and back on the jetty, they just ran the other way, around my outstretched arm and ended up behind me. I was now caught up in a ridiculous situation, for every duck I managed to persuade out of the boat, another two jumped in. I was now helpless with laughter and pleading with these insane avian to leave me in peace. I was just giving the two mother ducks who now were also aboard Mole, a stern talking to about their parental responsibilities, when I realised my antics were being observed closely by two passing canoeists. Noting their consternation, I tried to explain that I was being harassed by crazy ducks, but realising I must have sounded equally nuts, I just smiled. The pair continued to drift past, neither paddling nor averting their stare. I visualised them putting a call into the RSPB at the first opportunity, reporting some manic to be torturing poor little helpless ducks.

To be honest, I could have quite happily played the duck game for hours, but I was concerned about the distance I had to travel and needed to get going. So it would have to be Plan B. Either the ducks would disembark or join me on a trip to Monmouth. With a gentle push off the jetty, Mole slowly moved backwards out into the river, but miraculously before he was taken by the current, all my feathered friends as if ordered to abandoned ship, made a lemming-like evacuation over Mole's gunwales into the safety of the still water. As Mole was drawn away by the flow, I anxiously scanned the faster-flowing water passing the end of the jetty to see if any of the smaller fowl had been taken by the current, but saw none. Now the whole flush seemed to be safe and back on the jetty and being unperturbed, returned to playing one of their frenzied games. I'd been totally captivated by these amazing little fowl and a little sad to leave them. I'm sure without the photographic and video evidence no one would ever believe the games we played.

With frivolities over I slewed Mole around and set up a steady rate with the oars. It was another bright day with an ideal gentle breeze. The Wye was again broad and powerful, looking magnificent against the tree-covered escarpment of Park Wood on the right. My map indicated a sizeable industrial complex somewhere on the left bank at Stowfield, but fortunately it was obscured from view by the riverside bushes and trees. As the river began its loop to the left, I encountered the skeletal remains of yet another rail bridge, which according to my OS map, would have delivered trains immediately into the lengthy tunnel passing north under Park Wood towards Kerne Bridge.

Low-lying tilled land replaced the woodland as the Wye straightened out. I was joined by my first canoeists of the day, a pleasant family who told of their plans to lunch a few miles ahead at Symonds Yat. I was feeling quite warm so set about removing a layer of clothing and promptly banged and scraped through some less-than-shallow shallows that I'd failed to spot. Cursing my lack of diligence and not without further horrible grinding sounds, Mole was returned to deeper water. The river turned right with English Bicknor being somewhere up on higher ground to the left. English Bicknor is another interesting village and worthy of exploration by anyone walking the nearby Wye Valley Trail or Offa's Dyke. The village or hamlet's St. Mary the Virgin, is a Grade 1 listed Norman church with Saxon origins and stands in the courtyard of a once Norman motte and bailey castle.

After approximately five hundred yards the river dog-legged left, giving me my first view of the striking limestone pillars of Symonds Yat rocks, rising some four hundred feet. Nearing the cliffs I noted a number of unidentified raptors circling effortless at a relatively low level. Eventually I was directly underneath the flight and treated to an amazing aerial display performed by four red kites. Shipping the oars, I lay back to make the most of the opportunity. The kites came so low before climbing to catch the next thermal and even at some forty-plus feet above, I could see an amazing amount of detail. I was staggered by the deep tawny, red earth shade of their plumage and how the light-coloured under-feathers of their wings and tails flashed white when caught by the bright sun as they banked left or right. I could have watched the kites for hours, but as their circuits progressed up stream and the current took Mole downstream, they soon became indistinguishable against the dark background of trees and bushes growing upon the cliffs.

Without doubt, the Wye never failed to provided amazing experiences. Upon taking up the oars again, I had a painful reminder that I needed to improve the padding between my rear end and the hard marine plywood seating. To the thin foam-filled cushion and folded towel, I added a carefully folded sweatshirt, which for the moment seemed to improve matters. I'd been so absorbed in studying the imposing heights of limestone on my right, that upon giving my left side a cursory glance, I was somewhat surprised to find myself almost nose to nose with a large red and white cow, standing knee deep in the river. I quickly withdrew my left oar and reverse paddled with the right, which enabled me to just avoid colliding with the mighty beast. I was so close I could have patted the bemused-looking animal on the forehead.

Fortunately my course correction had also enabled the avoiding of the second unseen cow also taking the waters. Next over my left shoulder came a chap I presumed to be the farmer, who was carrying out remedial work upon the riverside fence. The perplexed look this gent gave me, suggested he was more than a little puzzled as to why I should be so close to his cows, given the river was about thirty yards wide at this point. Nevertheless, before I received any derogatory comments, I decided to compliment the fellow upon his fine Hereford stock and following a some amazing oar work managed to extract Mole from the riverside shallows and return to the main flow. The vision of two fine Herefords standing in the river was without doubt 'picturesque' and would have made a worthy study for the likes of John Constable, so I captured the enchanting 'cows in water' scene with my camera.

Reflecting upon on this occurrence sometime later, I was still amazed that the great beast seemed totally unperturbed at nearly being rammed by a lump of blue and white fibreglass. I know Herefords are renowned for their gentle nature, but I was still surprised that the animal had allowed Mole and myself to virtually pass under its nose without the slightest reaction. The day had already provided memorable and amusing encounters with ducks, red kites and cows. What would be next I wondered?

Drifting onwards, I scanned the towering heights of limestone trying to spot the Symonds Yat Rock view point, famed for providing picturesque views over the Wye, along with those of nesting and soaring peregrine falcons. Whilst gazing upwards, I unwittingly drifted among a flock of Canada geese. These majestic fowl seemed more aloof to my presence than bothered, allowing me to observe their striking black and white head plumage up close, which I also photographed. I was surprised to see a large swan happily paddling amidst this amicable geese armada.

Returning again to scanning the cliffs, I remembered reading that Iron Age inhabitants of 2,500 years ago, had built a fort upon the Symonds Yat cliff top, as it obviously made for an excellent vantage point. I also remember reading that the remains of the fort's earthworks are now protected as Scheduled Ancient Monument. As the river straightened out, the narrow cliff tops lowered into the rounded mound of Huntsham Hill, which interestingly has a number of caves or rock shelters on the northern side, where various artefacts believed to be from the late Mesolithic period were unearthed. From Huntsham Hill the land falls away to Huntsham Court the site of a Roman villa and Huntsham Court Farm, which is still owned and farmed by a descendant of the Vaughan family, who took up residence at the nearby Courtfield Manor in 1562.

On the right the tree-covered escarpment of Coppet Hill made for a stunning scene, climbing up as it did to a hilltop common nature reserve, of one hundred hectares. The Wye now began a gentle turn to the left as it approached the top or north end of the large Huntsham loop and I passed under the gentle arc of steel and cast iron that is the Grade II listed Hunsham Bridge. Since 1891 the bridge has provided access to Goodrich, Kerne Bridge and beyond. I was always fascinated by how the meandering Wye with its continuous looping, progressed little in linear terms. It had been almost twenty-four hours since I lunched at Kerne Bridge and now, as the river looped back again, Goodrich and Kerne Bridge were just a short walk away along the nearby B4229.

While mentally dealing with this conundrum, I came upon a familiar group of hikers sat taking a break upon the riverbank. I had first encountered my hiker friends the previous evening, when they stopped for a chat at my tent when tramping through the Welsh Bicknor campsite. They had apparently detoured from the conventional Wye Valley route in order to inspect the 'Queen Stone', a deeply grooved seven-foot stone monolith stood on the far side of the field, as some locals they met earlier, suggested the stone to be worthy of a visit. My new friends suggested that I should join them in visiting the 'Queen Stone', but I declined their kind invitation, citing that I was seriously behind schedule. So after wishing them good luck, I pulled away but not before pouring a cup of coffee from my flask and grabbing a medium-sized lump of flapjack.

The river turned left as it rounded the top of its loop and then straightened out before curving right and left as it approached to the two Symonds Yats of West and East. I was looking forward to seeing these two minor habitations, as I remembered being fascinated by their quaint riverside inns, hotels and such on a previous visit many years before. The strange name of Symonds Yat, is apparently derived from a seventeenth-century sheriff of Hereford called Robert Symonds and the 'Yat' bit was a contemporary term for 'gate or pass'.

Both swans and canoe hire traffic increased as I neared Symonds Yat West, which initiated a number of brief but congenial exchanges. I slowed my progress and spun Mole around to watch a red punt-like ferry making a river crossing. This interesting event was achieved by the ferryman pulling himself and therefore the ferry and four passengers across the Wye, by means of a thick rope spanning the river. It occurred that perhaps for hundreds of years, Wye ferries had been propelled back and forth in this manner. It was, I supposed, better than rowing, as the ferry was attached to the cross-river rope by a tether and ring, which slid freely along the rope as the ferryman pulled hand over hand. With this device, the ferry was permanently affixed to the rope and therefore less likely to be swept away down river in times of strong currents.

On the right-hand bank stood 'Ye Old Ferrie Inn', a very fine-looking fifteenth-century hostelry. I enviously noted a number of the inn's patrons on the riverside patio engrossed in studying the lunchtime menus, as I was thinking of food again. At this juncture, I suddenly remembered an arrangement made with my younger son Adam, that upon arriving at Symonds Yat West I would call him, so he could see me via the internet, as Symonds Yat West was the position of the second River Wye webcam.

I called Adam and held station while he found the appropriate website. Quite quickly the Symonds Yat webcam image appeared but Adam could not see me. I told him to wait for the image to refresh and he would see Mole next to the red rope ferry and me waving. To my consternation Adam confirmed he could see a green rope ferry, but not Mole! Eventually, the realisation dawned that I was at the wrong Symonds Yat, confirmed by my route notes, which correctly stated the webcam being at the Rose Cottage Tea Room, Symonds Yat East and not Ye Old Ferrie at Symonds Yat West. Somewhat sheepishly I confessed I'd got the wrong end of Symonds Yat and told Adam to leave the page open and I would call him back shortly.

Having weaved my way through river cruisers more swans and more hired canoes, I eventually covered the half mile to Symonds Yat East. I pressed the redial button on my mobile phone and Adam answered, but still could not see me. While I held station opposite the Rose Cottage Tea Room the webcam image refreshed and there I was there! We chatted briefly and said goodbye.

The white riverside buildings of Symonds Yat East looked equally as fabulous in the midday sun as did the West bit. I was now being seriously tempted by the offerings at the Rose Cottage Tea Garden and the Saracen's Head Inn, but pragmatism won out and so I set up a good rate with the oars. Without doubt, Symonds Yat was the best place I'd encountered so far for riverside hostelries that could be easily accessed by the river, just simply tie up, step out, place an order and enjoy. I decided that sometime in the future, I would return and spend a few days just sitting by the river at one or other of the hostelries, while partaking of the local wares and fayres. With the rope ferries, cruise boats and canoes it was an ideal place for my favourite pastime of water watching or 'gongoozling', a derisory term once used by bargees to describe the activity undertaken by those idlers with nothing better to do than hang around watching canal activity. I maintained my good rate with the oars, while watching

Symonds Yat slowly disappear in the distance.

Wooded land rose sharply to a good height on both sides of the river and from behind me I could hear the shouts and shrieks of excited youngsters. I took a cursory glance over my shoulder and caught sight of a mid-river island and lots of canoes. I checked my guide notes to identify this possible landmark and had a real major panic. I was now rapidly approaching my would-be nemesis, the dreaded Symonds Yat Rapids! To the seasoned canoeist these Grade II rapids would be considered very tame particularly at this time of the year, but to me they were definitely terrifying. Some years earlier the British Canoe Union had established these rapids as a white-water training facility and had built walls and positioned large boulders to create the desired waves and eddies.

I immediately spun Mole around to get a better view and worked the oars hard to slow my progress. Getting nearer, I could see clearly the surging, undulating water form white waves as it raced and reared up over unseen obstacles. I tried to identify a safe passage, but it all looked very scary. Near to the left bank above the rapids, I spotted a canoeist holding station in an eddy, while authoritatively encouraging a procession of canoeing youngsters as they approached and descended the foaming run. This chap was obviously knowledgeable so trying to sound calm, I enquired about the safest passage down and was advised to "stick to the middle". I spun Mole back around just in time, as the current took a firm hold and began to hurtle us towards disaster. I had visions of my dead body, an upturned boat and all my possessions being swept off down river and out to sea.

I decided the best action for keeping Mole on a straight course down the middle and not ending up going down the rapids sideways or backwards out of control, was to row hard and fast. I was now in the grips of a surging, seething, snarling monster, but found to my total amazement, that what I had expected to be a death-defying, white-knuckle ride turned out to be nothing more than a very exhilarating and most enjoyable experience. Mole, due to being heavily laden, just porpoised his way down the undulating course in a very dignified manner. He didn't scrape or bang against anything and with the flow being so directional, not once was a course correction required. There were times when I thought that the white-water waves were higher than Mole's gunnels, but not a drop came over.

At the bottom pool I pulled to the side and found an eddy where I could ship the oars, relax and take stock. I was euphoric and really wished I could do it all over again. Although these rapids were only considered to be a Grade II run and therefore deemed suitable for canoeing beginners, one could not help but be impressed with the sheer power and acceleration of the water. I was equally surprised by the height differential between the top and bottom of the rapids; this gradient along with the artificial narrowing obviously created the considerable increase in both flow and power. I also remember looking down into the water mid-passage and being surprised by how the aeration had been given the water a light greenish hue.

I hadn't conquered Niagara or the Grand Canyon, but even so I was quite pleased with myself for overcoming one of my main two concerns about the whole trip; now I was just left with the murderous mud at Chepstow to contend with. I decided the moment was worthy of celebration, so toasted my achievement with the remnants of my flask, a quarter mug of lukewarm coffee. I spent a moment or two watching the many young canoeists enjoying the spectacle of the rapids. Some just sat and chatted as they watched others, who having made it down safely would repeatedly land, carry their canoes back to the top and come hurtling down again. I had to congratulate the British Canoe Union, this was an ideal resource for developing the interest, skills and character of youngsters.

Before my adrenaline-fuelled euphoria faded I set off downriver again, watching as I went the endless chain of yellow and red canoes tumble down the white water, all under the eyes of their ever-vigilant instructors. It was a nice bright day, with uplifting large areas of blue sky. Again the Wye was magnificent as it ran through a deep wooded ravine, with almost sheer sides rising a few hundred feet up to Mailscot Wood on the left and Lord's Wood on the right. Lord's Wood was not only the site of the Great Doward Caves, of which the largest being King Arthur's Cave, but perhaps more interesting, is that Lord's Wood also boasts an ancient settlement where flint tools were discovered, along with the bones of reindeer, bears, hyenas and lions.

I was now more convinced than ever, that the only way to really discover and truly appreciate the full majesty of the Wye was to travel its serpentining extent by river craft. I considered the comparison between observing the Wye valley from the river and the views and panoramas that can only be seen from mountain peaks and for that reason, remain the preserve of those able to ascend the lofty heights. It is of little wonder, that this part of the Wye valley had been granted 'Area of Outstanding Natural Beauty' (AONB) status or that the likes of Thackeray, Wordsworth and Tuner in the late eighteenth century should have been so captivated by the Wye that they were compelled to exalt its virtues in words, verse and canvas.

Passing under Bibblins Bridge, a lightweight structure which apart from being a navigation aid to river travellers, provides pedestrian access to the nearby campsite, I reflected upon how the Wye had healed and recovered from all the wounds and ravages wreaked by the industrial age. Of course Coleridge, Wordsworth and the like were probably fortunate to enjoy the spectacular Wye landscape before the railways, coalmining and iron working reached its peak. Equally, from all accounts the early nineteenth-century Wye was no place for pleasure cruising, given the level of industrial cargo-carrying river traffic plying up and down. I thought the Wye to be reminiscent of my own birthplace, some eight miles west of Manchester, which has become a desirable and much sought-after place to live. Whereas in my early childhood, the village was surrounded by numerous coal mines, railways, cotton mills, canals and engineering works, which combined to pollute everything or at least covered everything in dirt and soot. But following gentrification, colliery sites have long since been landscaped into nature reserves, railways no longer with rails and sleepers now facilitate Sunday afternoon family strolls.

Due to being lost in thought, it was some while before it dawned that I was being hailed by someone. Looking around I saw a group of people calling and waving from the riverside. Eventually I realised it was my good friend Dominic and extended family from last night's campsite. As I had passed the group, it was a massive lung-busting effort to cross the flow and row back up stream to where the group sat lunching on a very pleasant stretch of beach. After running Mole aground next to the groups canoes, I lay back for a moment or two trying to catch my breath, which to my embarrassment Dominic photographed. Despite my protestations, the kind ladies insisted that I should partake of their pile of sandwiches. Dominic's sister-in-law apologised for not having the facilities to provide a drink other than water, but I did. So from Mole I retrieved my gas stove, kettle, five assorted drinking vessels and box with all the necessary ingredients. I soon had the four adults of the party plied with tea and coffee as my contribution to the feast. Being conscious of the time, after thirty minutes or so of pleasant chat, I thanked my kind hosts and set off downriver.

Having completed its right-hand loop, the river began its slow turn to the left and then ran almost straight for a while. The tree-covered land still rose sharply from the riverbank on both sides. My map indicated that the Seven Sisters Rocks and King Arthur's Cave should be somewhere up on the right. I could see some rocks, but whether it was the Seven Sisters I couldn't confirm. Up on the left somewhere out of my view stood the more interesting sounding Far Hearkening Rock. According to sources, this lump of rock is unusual for the area as it is formed of dolomite and has served numerous rulers, royal, Roman and Welsh tribal as an observation point. I was now approaching Hadnock Island, which my guide advised to pass on the less weedy left side. The island was small but would have made for an nice place to cook a meal or camp overnight, but more importantly the island served to indicate that I had less than three miles to my camp at Monmouth.

My increasingly painful rear end and swollen ankles were another conundrum. Rowing normally with my feet down on Mole's hull was just about bearable with the amount of padding I was sat on, but this position caused my ankles to swell up. Rowing with my feet up on the seating reduced the swelling, but transferred more weight upon my rear end, which then became more painful. I had already increased the pile of towels and clothing as padding but to no avail. I decided that my only option was to tie the sausage-like dry bag which contained my soft sleeping bag and airbed to my seat and sit on it. What a relief, it was excellent. It did feel strange at first as I felt to be sitting much higher up, but in reality it was only three inches once the bag flattened out.

With the distraction of pain gone, I concentrated on making progress with the oars. Like many days on the Wye, the weather seemed to improve in the late afternoon. The tree-covered steep slopes of the left-hand bank were replaced by arable land which gently rolled down to the river in the bright afternoon sunshine. The river took a slight curve right before making a tight left turn and then suffered from the parallel proximity of the busy A40 cross-Wales trunk road. Although I couldn't see the A40 I could hear it! A youngish chap in a skiff shot past me and after fifty yards or so turned around and flew past the other way, so I knew I was nearing Monmouth Rowing Club. This was now a very straight section of the river, ideal for rowing events, and I caught my first sight of the rather fine red sandstone five-arch bridge dating from 1615.

Passing Monmouth Rowing Club, I presented the assembled patrons with a plausible impression of fine blademanship and was soon up to and under the grand bridge carrying the A466 over the Wye. I remembered to check my guide as I had written down explicit instructions provided by the Monnow Bridge Campsite staff upon how to reach my next overnight stop. So having passed under the Wye bridge I had to look for the confluence of the River Monnow on the right. Once under the bridge, the River Wye runs even closer to the A40 before bending left and after roughly half a mile the Wye is joined by the Monnow. My first impressions were that the River Monnow was little more than a shallow stream, for as I turned in all I could see was large islands of small stones with a narrow ribbon of shallow water wandering between. I was amused that the town of Monmouth should gain its name from this little river. I was next instructed to pass under the bridge and would find the campsite access on the left.

I finally capitulated and gave up any intentions of rowing the Monnow, after repeatedly having to get out and push every few yards and instead, opted for wading knee-deep all the way to Monmouth, while pulling Mole behind me. To navigate the occasional pools of unfathomable depth, I would sit upon Mole's foredeck and punt across with an oar.

It was somewhat ironic that I should reprise Humphrey Bogart's role in one of my all-time favourite films, 'The African Queen'. The number of times I'd relished Bogart and Hepburn's battle against the odds as they travelled down a treacherous river in a small boat called the 'African Queen', in order to sink a WWI German gunboat patrolling Lake Tanganyika. However, just before reaching the lake, their boat becomes mired by dense reeds and mud, requiring Bogart to get into the water and tow it through leech-infested water. Although I didn't think the Monnow was leech infested, the reality of my plight was far from glamorous, especially as I was stubbing my toe upon unseen boulders every few yards.

I eventually passed under the bridge which carried the A40 but saw no campsite access on the left or in fact anything, either left or right. Somewhat perplexed I checked my map and the map in my guide book, but neither scale was big enough to help in any way. I thought perhaps the campsite maybe close by but I just couldn't see it from the river. After a sudden flash of inspiration, I retrieved my mobile phone from its waterproof case and having confirmed that I had a suitable signal strength, contacted the site for better directions.

The phone was answered by a young girl of undeterminable age. I explained that I had followed their instructions to find the site and had passed under the bridge as I had been directed, but couldn't see the camp. I was then told that the site was just behind the white buildings on the end of the bridge. Having stated that there were no white buildings on either end of this bridge, the was a prolonged silence. The girl then asked if my bridge had a small house on it, to which I answered in the negative. After another silence the girl said I was obviously at the wrong bridge and I needed the old bridge further on near the town, which had three arches and a little house on top.

Then the girl dropped the bombshell, "You'll have to carry your canoe over the big stones just before the bridge," she said. Very slowly and calmly I asked the girl to clarify what she meant by "big stones" and "carry my canoe". The girl restated that to even get to the aforementioned bridge, it would be necessary to somehow get over the row of very large stones that spanned the river.

It would be inappropriate for me to reproduce the tirade of abuse that I rent upon this poor girl, but she did admit to receiving my booking call and did remember me enquiring about ease of site access because of my craft type and health issues. I was very annoyed, tired and not feeling very well due to missing my afternoon nap and now I had to overcome some major obstacle just to get to my campsite. I resolved to reach this stone obstruction and if it was insurmountable, then I would find a suitable place to tie up Mole and I would spend the night aboard. In fact, the prospect of this second option lifted my spirits considerably; after all, I had initially considered and facilitated this possibility. I had all the food and water I needed, I could blow up my airbed, get in my sleeping bag and use the tent flysheet as a waterproof cover. What could be better?

Before setting off, I refuelled with a beaker of cider and a lump of flapjack and after walking up the River Monnow for about half an hour, I eventually approached the rather magnificent Monnow Bridge complete with gatehouse. Some forty feet before, the dreaded large stones stretched across the river. I beached Mole in the shallows and weighed up my predicament. It appeared that centuries earlier large blocks of sandstone had been laid across the river to create what I presumed to be a weir or crossing point. At either side of the river, the stones created a much wider causeway and were between one and two feet above the water level. In the middle, the stones were laid in a single row and much lower, probably due to being worn away by the endless passage of water. Therefore the outer and wider stones funnelled the main flow of the river over an eight-foot section of the middle and lower blocks.

My first option was to float Mole over to the right-hand side of the crossing, unload all my stuff then pull or push Mole up on top of the stones, then drag him some ten feet across the short causeway to the other side, where he would be put back into the river and reloaded. Although dragging an unloaded Mole over the ten feet of stone causeway would be relatively easy, the actual route to approach the big stones was obstructed by slightly smaller, randomly placed stones which would be extremely difficult to manoeuvre over. My second option would be to push Mole over the lower central section of the stones, using the oncoming water flow to provide some floatation over the almost submerged stones. There wasn't a place to stand and pull Mole up and over by his painter, as the crossing acted as a weir, therefore the water on the other side of the stones was far too deep to be of any use. I tested the pool in front of the central section and discovered I would need to be at least waist deep in water to be in the right position push Mole up and over. So by standing up to my midriff in water, I was near enough to establish that the depth of water flowing over the stones was enough to help but not too much to push against. So it was going to be option two.

Wading out of the pool, I noticed that a number of people had now stopped on the bridge to observe the antics of the mad man below. Back at Mole I grabbed my camera to record the situation, as nobody would ever believe that anybody would be insane enough to try pushing a sailing dinghy up a waterfall, but it was an adventure after all. Having returned my camera to its waterproof bag, I pushed

Mole out into the pool, lined him up with the lower section stones and took up my position at the stern.

The nearer I pushed Mole to the stones the more the resistance the water flow increased, but not enough to overpower me. I was now waist deep again and if I pushed Mole any nearer to the stones, the water flow would come over the bow and into the boat. Realising that Mole's bow was too low to ride up the flow, I both pushed down on the transom to lift the bow and forward with all my might at the same time. It worked, Mole's bow lifted sufficiently to ride up the flow and was now resting upon the stones. I repeated the same action and slid Mole further on top of the stones. I daren't release my forward pressure or the water would have pushed Mole back into the pool. Just one more effort would have Mole balanced on top on the stones I hoped. I paused to recover and catch my breath and looking up, saw that my audience now spanned the entire length of the bridge and oddly, most of them seemed to be eating ice creams.

It was now or never, before my little remaining strength disappeared forever. Either my last big effort would see Mole balanced on top of the stones, only needing a little shove to have him into the deep water or, once the entire hull was exposed to the full force of the water I would be no longer be able to hold him and both of us would end up back in the pool. So after a few deep breaths, I steadied myself and lifted Mole's stern while pushing forward with every ounce of my strength. Mole seem to hesitate, then slid forward but much further than expected and ended up more than halfway over, with his keel just about resting on the middle stone. Satisfied Mole wouldn't be swept back over if I let go, I grabbed the painter and nonchalantly walked out of the side of the pool, climbed up onto the stones nearer the bank and from that angle just ahead of Mole's bow managed to pull him into the deeper water. Totally buoyant again, Mole bobbed around in the current; I easily guided him to a suitable spot and climbed aboard.

To my surprise, my loyal and appreciative audience acknowledged my great endeavour with a polite round of applause, so I stood up a gave a gracious bow. Still being observed, I took up the oars and set up an orderly rate as I passed under and out the other side of the bridge, continuing until I had covered the fifty yards or so, to the supposed landing place for the Monnow Bridge Campsite. I tied

Mole's painter to a convenient piece of ironwork and lay full length in the boat and closed my eyes; I was totally shattered and very wet. I was close to falling asleep where I was, but rallied myself as I still had many things to do, of which the first was to sort my campsite out. I pulled Mole nearer to the short flight of decrepit stone steps and scrambled up the bank. It took a while to fathom the route, which led along the riverbank then up and over and down a five-foot stone wall by means of concrete staircase, then across the campsite to the office. If I was annoyed about having to carry Mole over the big stones, I was fuming about having to carry all my stuff up and over a commando course.

The office was closed, so following the instructions written upon a faded piece of paper Sellotaped to the door, I rang the bell. After my second and much prolonged pressing of the bell, the proprietor appeared at an opened upstairs window. Whether this chap was expecting to receive a severe rant so remained out of harm's way I wasn't sure. Therefore I played a bad tempered Romeo to his Juliet, repeating my well-practised spleen venting upon the incredulity, of having specifically enquired about and explained my necessity for an easy access to and from the river. Then to find, not only did I have to manhandle my boat over a mid-river major obstacle, but lug all my camping equipment over a military assault course.

Eventually I ceased hostilities and was allotted a piece of grass between and the aforementioned riverside wall and a vacant static caravan. I took the opportunity to familiarise myself with and use the facilities, which as I expected were poor.

"Blessed is he who expects little."
Attributed to many

Ambling back across the campsite in the general direction of Mole, I began formulating a plan for shuttling all my stuff between the river and my bit of grass. While lost in my deepest thoughts, a chap from a parked up campervan hailed my attention. Apparently he and his wife had been out for an afternoon stroll and had noticed me earlier passing Monmouth Rowing Club, then seeing me again pushing Mole over the stones and now there I was, walking past their van. They were fascinated and intrigued to know what I was about and I was amazed to know how they had recognised me. With amusement my new friends pointed out that I was still wearing a lifejacket, a fact I'd overlooked.

I decided that I couldn't refuse the offer from these nice people of a comfy chair, a cup of coffee and a slice of homemade fruit cake, in exchange for the telling of my tale. Having told my saga of the Wye we chatted back and forth on the merits of campervans, caravans and such. I will tell of my new friend's tale of woe concerning their horrendously expensive engine failure, due to using a non-approved replacement cambelt. So if they ever read this account, they'll recognise themselves and know I haven't forgotten their kind hospitality.

With improved spirits I returned to the river. Now back at Mole I had started to feel rather ill with fatigue. Pushing myself in this state could have detrimental effects, but I had no option. Remembering I'd stowed a can of high-energy caffeine drink in one of Mole's buoyancy compartments, I thought it would provide the needed boost while sorting out my stuff. My plan was to only carry the bare minimum needed to get through the night and leave the rest in Mole, as he was in a relatively safe place. I carried and erected my tent and bedding at a very sedate pace. Next trip was gas stove, kettle full of water and cup with tea bag etc., a ready-meal and pan. Into my pocket went the penultimate piece of flapjack from tin one and on my back went my rucksack of valuables. Before the effects of the energy drink started to wane, I quickly put on my night attire and for the first time, had supper in bed. I'd survived a very adventurous and although I wouldn't admit to the campsite staff, a very enjoyable day.

CHAPTER 11

Stones Again!

"There is no certainty; there is only adventure."
Roberto Assagioli

Checking my watch, I was moderately surprised that I'd managed twelve hours of deep refreshing sleep, but desperately needed to use the facilities. There wasn't time to cross the assault course and fetch my ablution kit from Mole, so it was a rather hurried cross-legged trip across the site. Upon my return trip I gave the site the once over. It was a small site and due to the number of campervans and caravans, it all looked a bit cramped. The site was next to the River Monnow and small nature meadow, but still retained the ambiance of a rather tired town centre site, which I suppose is what it was.

I downed and packed away the tent and transported everything back across the assault course, which due to my minimalistic approach of the previous evening was completed relatively easily. It was another nice warm morning so I set about preparing my porridge and coffee on the secluded riverbank just above Mole.

From my tree-covered grassy bank I was able to study the thirteenth-century Monnow gated bridge in all its glory. Local sources claim the bridge to be unique in the UK and only one of three such gated bridges remaining in Europe. Originally constructed for defensive purposes, the gatehouse was complete with portcullis and sentry rampart, but due to the Monnow being too shallow it proved ineffective. The little gatehouse had seen many uses, ranging from toll collection to private dwelling and in the interest of preservation, the bridge is now restricted to pedestrian use.

Here the river was about thirty feet or so wide and six or seven feet deep, due to the weir effect of the large stones just beyond the bridge. If I'd more time, I would have adventured further upstream. I knew the Monnow to be popular with canoeists and is claimed to be a beautiful touring river. The bank opposite was relatively steep and also had a stone wall running along which screened a number of buildings. It occurred that as the bridge was so near, I should use it to plan my return passage back over the dammed stones.

With all my equipment stowed and Mole readied for the off, I walked back across the site to the entrance, which opened onto a small road. Turning left I trundled sixty yards or so to a mini roundabout then turned left again towards the bridge. The small approach road boasted half a dozen nicely appointed retail establishments, which contributed to the overall pleasing visual effect, especially with the bridge gatehouse in the background. Just standing on the bridge was quite pleasant, I could understand why so many people had lingered as they promenaded the previous evening.

Looking down on the rocks, I was surprised by the overnight change in water level. Now there was far more water and some of the stones I had stood on previously to pull Mole over into the deeper water, had disappeared. I could easily imagine thrashing white water barrelling over this weir in winter times. Given that there was now far more water pouring over the central section of the crossing, I was confident that without my weight, Mole would easily return over the stones the way he came.

I retraced my steps rather wearily and climbed aboard Mole. After checking everything was tied down I gave the notes concerning the next nine miles to my camp at Tintern Old Station a quick read, then slowly set off towards the bridge. Passing out from under the bridge, I spun Mole around and approached the line of stones near the riverbank backwards. Fortunately the higher water had created a useful eddy, which allowed me to manoeuvre next to a big stone and climb out. My aim was to push Mole backwards towards the bridge, then guide his approach to the centre stones with the bow and stern lines. With Mole lined up and pointing in the right direction, he eventually began to move as the current took hold and slowly carried him towards the overflow. I released the stern line but kept hold of the bow line as I clambered over the stones and waded back into the downstream pool, which was also deeper. As Mole started to pass over the weir I began to pull hard on the bow line. The overflow appeared to be carrying Mole over the stones. Just as he was almost over, the very end of the keel section caught on a stone, momentarily causing Mole to nose dive into the pool, before levelling out and bobbing around quite happily. If only getting him up and over the night before had been that easy, I mused.

The Monnow's additional water certainly improved my passage downstream. This, combined with the bright sunlight, sparkling on the water as it passed over the gravel shallows, provided a good start to the day's journey, apart from being extremely wet. Once out and back on my old friend the Wye, I started a sedate pace with the oars. Again the river looked wide, deep and resplendent, as the bright morning sun shone upon the broadleaves of the tall riverside trees. After a short distance, I passed under and by the remains of another two former railway bridges. The first being a single span of red rust steel, whereas the second was missing its cross-river span, but did retain a number of splendid stone arches that approached the river on either side. Considering the bridges, I was sure the Wye must hold the world record for the river having the most disused railway bridges. Apparently, I should have looked out for large underwater obstructions, remaining from the bridges' demolition, I belatedly learned from my guide.

As a navigational note, I'd written a reminder about the confluence of the River Trothy on the right. This minor tributary I found to be similar to the Monnow, as it joined the Wye in a very modest way. I could imagine a much different situation in the full flood of winter, as the Trothy would become quite a monster with all the water collected as it travelled down from its rising point northeast of Abergavenny to the Wye at Monmouth.

I was sure that the amount of waterborne wildlife was diminishing the further down the river I travelled. Days earlier, I had to virtually cut a swath through swans, ducks, geese and fish, but now it was hard to find any. Through the trees on the left I could see some major constructions, which my map confirmed to be a sewage works, but I preferred not to think about its close proximity to the river. As the

Wye took a left turn, I came upon my first canoeists of the day, a couple of teenagers enjoying the river and much to my relief, a family of ducks.

After a while the Wye took a ninety-degree turn right. The sky now had all but a few clouds and it was getting rather warm. The sun was starting to burn through my thinning pate, so I sought and stuck on my guaranteed UV-resistant bush hat and applied sunscreen to my other exposed skin. My shorts, once soggy from my earlier wading had virtually dried out, so all was well in my world. Beyond the right-hand bank, the land progressively and pleasantly rose up to the village of Penallt, which unsurprisingly translates from the Welsh as 'top of wooded hill'. Penallt also enjoys a twelfth-century church and seventeenth-century pub. On the left, the A466 now ran in close proximity, but fortunately the infrequent traffic did not ruin the tranquillity.

The river flow noticeably increased, which I attributed to the additional waters from the Monnow and Trothy, so I spun Mole around, relaxed and drifted backwards for a while. It was at such times I could really appreciate the natural beauty of the Wye. I remembered the good William Gilpin in his eighteenth-century work *Observations on the Wye*, mentioning this particularly stretch of river and describing *"boats with white sails passing along woodland hills"* as picturesque. However, Gilpin contrasts his picturesque visions with those of *"small bays and harbours, where rough working boats load and unload ore and other such cargoes"*.

With my period of reflection over, I swung Mole back around and saw I was being overhauled by a trio of canoes stuffed with youngsters. With a couple of strokes of the oars I'd made way for my fellow river travellers, who the rather harassed-looking young lady instructor told me, were shortly leaving the river at the village of Redbrook, which I gathered couldn't come too soon. I let the canoes draw a good distance ahead before taking up the oars. The river maintained its relatively straight course, with tall broadleaved riverside trees affording much welcomed shade. While taking a quick over-shoulder glance for navigational purposes, I spotted another steel bridge spanning the river ahead.

This ex-railway bridge crossed the river diagonally, therefore passing between its eight cylindrical steel piers required attention. It would have been fun watching the giant Dutch barge back at Hereford squeeze through these bridge supports. I was pleased to note the bridge was at least still being used by pedestrians, as I returned the waves from a family in hiking garb passing overhead.

The three canoes I'd followed, pulled into the left-hand bank a short distance ahead. My map confirmed this to be the Lower of the two Redbrooks, which according to my guide was where the last act of piracy on the Wye took place. It seems that two barges were captured by felons from the nearby Forrest of Dean. As these were obviously dangerous parts, I needed to be extra vigilant. Lower Redbrook benefits from shops and inns, so it made for a good opportunity to replenish my depleted stock of lemonade. Nearing the canoeists, I asked one of the instructors about the proximity of the shops and leant to my good fortune, that there was a shop and Post Office just a few yards from the riverbank, on the other side of the road. As the water level was far below the riverbank, I couldn't see anything beyond. I held station while the young crews disembarked and clambered up the riverbank, pulling up the canoes after them.

Lower Redbrook wasn't blessed with an ideal access point from the river. There was a stone construction further on, probably a leftover quay from centuries before, but it was now overgrown with trees and bushes and also, far too high to be of any help to me. My only option was to land where the canoes had beached, so I donned my small rucksack and precariously make my way up the almost vertical riverbank. Eventual I scaled the bank and after pausing to catch my breath and take in the view, I ambled about fifty yards across a nicely mown piece of grass to where the Redbrook Post Office and Village Store stood on the far side of the A466.

Once inside, I spotted the soft drink stock towards the rear of the shop. Having selected a two-litre bottle of pop I made my way to the patiently awaiting lady shopkeeper at the till. Upon passing the fresh food refrigerator, my eyes fell upon a rather large, plump and delicious-looking Cornish pasty, which I just could not resist. I had a tin of marrowfat peas which would make for the perfect accompaniment, together with a good dollop of tomato sauce and sliced pickled beetroot of course. Heating the beast was going to be a problem, but I would resolve that difficulty later.

Having completed my purchases and left the shop, I thought I'd stretch my legs a little and see if could get a better look at the old quay or what I thought to be an old quay. So crossed the road back into the gentrified area of riverside, complete with manicured grass, tarmac pathways and benches. Interestingly, the focal point of this public garden was a large bronze disc set in the ground, some six feet or so in diameter. Around the circumference in large raised type it stated 'Redbrook Village Green' and in the centre an image in relief, depicting Redbrook's significant metal-working heritage. This was a fine monument.

Looking around, it was hard to believe that this tranquil little village had witnessed such industrial pandemonium, as generated by iron furnaces, copper and tin-plate working, flour milling and brewing until 1962. It was even more amazing to consider that as early as the fifteenth century raw material and finished produce would have arrived and been transported from the very quay just a few yards from where I stood. Of course, arrival of the Wye valley railway in 1876 would seriously diminish river transportation to and from Redbrook. Further exploration found the old quay to be as equally inaccessible from the village green as it was from the riverside.

With legs sufficiently stretched, I ambled back to Mole, precariously made my way down the riverbank, climbed aboard and cast off. I adopted my ankle anti-swelling position with my feet up on Mole's buoyancy tanks and incurred intense pain as the bare skin of my ankle came in contact with the red-hot fibreglass. The strong power of the late morning sun had made the white fibreglass virtually untouchable, which gave me a great idea for heating my Cornish pasty. I fished out my deep aluminium pan, dropped in my luscious pasty, replaced the lid and positioned it in the direct sunlight next to Mole's gunnels.

The river continued majestically through a series of small, meandering, tree-lined valleys, still followed closely by the A466 road. I exchanged brief pleasantries with a couple of hikers seeking shade under a riverside tree, before continuing along the Wye valley path to lunch at the nearby village of Whitebrook. On the right, above the resting hikers was Hael Wood, which I later discovered was a semi-ancient woodland and a Site of Special Scientific Interest, due to its 'biological characteristics'. What these characteristics were, I never discovered. A gentle breeze countered the burning sun. I was torn between seeking shade from the tall riverside trees and keeping my pasty-heating solar oven in direct sunlight. I was surprised by how warm my pasty had become, but whether it had heated all the way through was another question.

I passed by the village Whitebrook which was roughly halfway to my next overnight at the Old Station, Tintern, so it was time to find a place to stop for lunch. Open farmland replaced the riverside trees and suitable stopping places began to appear. I came upon an ideal spot to beach Mole, with a comfortable-looking grass-covered bank to sit upon. I ran Mole ashore and shipped the oars and after repositioning my solar oven in direct sunlight, I set up the gas stove and heated a pan of marrowfat peas. With much trepidation, I stuck a fork into the middle of my mighty pasty and withdrew a sample, which was as I suspected a little on the cool side. In hindsight, I should have dismissed any thought of heating the beast, as I had now probably rendered it inedible. Refusing to be beaten, I cut the west country speciality in half, then sliced the halves longitudinally. I placed two of the quarters innards downwards into my oiled wok, covered with a lid and placed on the gas stove.

Eventually the object of my gastronomic desire reached post-botulism temperatures. Although with all the testing and anti-stick manoeuvring that my pride and joy had endured, it no longer resembled its previous mouth-watering form. However, once partnered with the marrowfat peas, pickled beetroot and doused with tomato sauce, it surpassed all expectations. I subjected the remaining quarters to my questionable heating procedure and downed the lot.

"Being far away from civilization our victualling was all done aboard our craft each day, and lunch and tea were important functions, and very enjoyable they were under such picnic conditions."

P. Bonthron

While finishing off my after-lunch cup of tea I surveyed my surroundings. The Wye had changed again; no longer deep, wide and powerful, but shallow and gentle. Sitting upon the soft grassy bank brought welcomed relief to my painful rear end and I was just enjoying my location when the mood was shattered by a very noisy two-stroke motorbike, across the river, on the now very close A466. I hadn't realised the close proximity of the main road, but apart from that, I liked the open aspect of this spot. The sun was directly overhead and burning holes in me, so it was totally unsuitable for my much-needed siesta. So I propelled Mole back out into midstream and set off in search of riverside shade.

I couldn't believe it! I must have passed a million riverside trees on my journey so far, but now there wasn't even one tree, bush or blade of grass capable of protecting me from the sun. Bizarrely, I next encountered nineteen very large black, brown and white bulls, who had come down the steep riverbank to take the waters. Half of these giant bovines were stood shoulder to shoulder a good way out into the river and eyed me menacingly. I decided to risk being drowned by rampaging bulls and paused just a few yards away to record the spectacle with my camera.

With the eventual appearance of the elegant single-arch span of Bigsweir Bridge, came tall, broadleaf, riverside trees. I selected a suitable spot of shade and tied Mole's painter around an exposed root. I reckoned within an hour, Mole's bow would no longer be in the shade, so opted to nap with my head at the stern, and arranged my boxes and softer items accordingly. After quickly applying sunscreen to my exposed skin, I settled down and pulled my hat over my face.

I regained consciousness almost an hour later, but as I was extremely comfortable decided to stay where I was until fully awake. As my head was virtually hanging over the stern, I could spy out sideways from under my hat. My gaze fixed upon what I presumed to be a mayfly engaged in metamorphosis. Being no more than a foot and a half from my head on the surface of the river, I had a perfect view of this transformation and was particularly fascinated having never seen this marvel so close before.

It was special to witness the insect begin to climb out of the nymph of its previous incarnation and to aid its escape, the insect began to slowly flap its wings, which were light in colour and similar in size to that of a moth. Once free of the old form, the fly slowly ascended from the surface of the water to a height of approximately eight inches where it momentarily hovered.

I was just regretting not capturing this amazing metaphorical and ever so graceful manifestation with my camera's video facility, when a gigantic open-mouthed monster broke from the deep and after swallowing my new insect friend, returned from whence it came. For that split second, I'd looked that beast in the eye, tooth and scale. Whether this denizen of the deep had been a salmon or a sea trout I couldn't tell, but it was massive, probably in excess of fifteen pounds. However, regardless of its species or weight it gave me such a fright, that from my sleepy repose I virtually leaped to the other side of the boat.

I sat for a while, now wide awake, and reassured myself that what I thought had happened, had actually happened and it wasn't all a dream. The incident had left me with mixed emotions. I was both sad and angry that my poor mayfly after all that effort in performing such a miracle of nature, had its life snuffed out in seconds. I knew mayflies were known to be short-lived and were particularly vulnerable to birds or fish at this stage of their development, but even so it was all very sad.

Perhaps more worrying or at least more embarrassing, was my automatic response to the incident, for I actually exclaimed, "We've got to get a bigger boat!" In my defence for using such a hackneyed the film reference, I admit the fish was no 'Jaws', but defy anyone half asleep, not to experience a heart-stopping moment with the sudden appearance of a giant gaping salmon, just a few inches from the end of their nose. I untied Mole, took up the oars and considered my fears of rapids and mud had all been misdirected, as the wildlife of the Wye seemed to be far more intimidating.

Nearing Bigsweir Bridge, I was taken by the stunning mirror image reflected upon the water by this elegant cast-iron structure. The light blue painted latticed ironwork in bright sunlight was magnificent against the backdrop of billowy white clouds and rolling green hills. I drifted for a while to enjoy the vision and before getting underway, captured the image with my camera. I'd never seen a bridge so perfectly befitting to its location. Rather than compromising the picturesque, it actually enhanced it. I envisaged the engineer or architect who designed the fifty-five-yard single span back in 1827, had a keen eye for the artistic.

It would perhaps be wrong to berate our contemporary designers, schooled in steel and concrete, for their bland efforts by comparison, as generally their creations are constrained by load-bearing requirements and budget limitations, not facilitating imaginative designs. Equally, this stunning cast-iron edifice designed to carry the horse-drawn loads of the day, falls way short of current vehicle requirements and has to be restricted to traffic-light controlled, single-lane operation.

Shortly after the unrivalled Bigsweir Bridge disappeared from view, I spotted my next landmark, the village of Llandogo on the right-hand bank, rising up the wooded hillside. Here the Wye changed again, once more seeming deep, dark and slow moving. I mused over how I now propelled Mole with consummate ease; the oars entered and left the water with the minimum of disturbance. My green rubber-palmed work gloves had been excellent and maintained my hands in great condition, neither a blemish nor a blister after eight days of rowing. I wished I could find a similar solution for my rear end. Regardless of all the additional layers of padding, towards late afternoon of each day it became very painful.

The riverside had also changed. Overhanging trees once more reached down to dip the tips of their branches into the water. Their root systems exposed by repeated surging of high water, provided an excellent playground for small waterfowl with their young, who busily paddled in and around, playing 'follow-my-leader'. I was reminded that I hadn't yet seen a vole or water rat, which was disappointing for a life-long devotee of Kenneth Graham's *Wind in the Willows*.

From my musings, I became aware that I was keeping abreast of a pair of hikers maintaining a brisk pace along the riverside 'Offa's Dyke Path'. From our intermittent conversation carried on in the gaps between the trees and bushes, I learnt that the nice lady and gentleman were celebrating their thirtieth wedding anniversary by walking the 177-mile route. The nice lady complained of having to suffer her husband's fast walking pace and instead of enjoying a pleasant stroll through the countryside, he kept going at route march speed and moaned when she lagged behind. She went on to add with a wry smile, that it would be a miracle if they got to the end without her instigating divorce proceedings!

I picked up my own pace and bade my new companions farewell, as they marched onward to their overnight billet, which was apparently a few miles somewhere downriver. It never failed to amaze me, that when total strangers met on a mountain top, forest trail or even riverbank path, etiquette demands at least an enthusiastic greeting, but quite often an in-depth chat, like long-lost pals who quite readily exchange all sorts of personal information, whereas city dwellers, particularly our southern brethren I gather, barely speak to each other and avoid eye contact at all costs. I suppose it's the bond between like-minded people, who share a common interest in the great outdoors and a love of nature. One doesn't feel threatened by jolly folk in hiking gear, rucksacks and woolly hats halfway up a mountain, after all, no drug-crazed mugger is going to hike miles or climb several thousand feet in search of potential victims.

After some nine miles from Monmouth, I neared the small village of Llandogo nestling into the wooded hillside. The mainly white-painted buildings were captivating, as they appeared to have been positioned in an orderly terraced manner. While considering this riverside architecture I was almost caught out by a sudden increase in current as the river turned left. Just in time I identified the rapids and shallows to be avoided and steered towards the deeper but faster water. Once taken by the stronger current Mole sped along the curved passage carved in the river bedrock. The sudden acceleration and bouncing of the tumbling water was quite enjoyable. I was just thinking I had survived the rollercoaster ride, when Mole violently slammed side-on into some large unseen boulder and nearly pitched me overboard.

By the resulting loud crack, I was sure that Mole's hull must have split or at least, had a large hole punched in it. Not daring to look, I headed for the first available beach to carry out an inspection of Mole's underside. With much apprehension I stepped ashore and tied Mole up the nearest bush. Fearing the worst and being so annoyed that I had probably curtailed my adventure so close to its conclusion, I began checking the lower side Mole's white fibreglass hull. I saw nothing! Not a mark!

I tipped Mole over on his keel and maintained the position by jamming a suitably sized boulder under the hull. While at this angle, it was possible to visually inspect one side of Mole's hull from bow to stern. Given that it was quite possible for a crack or split in the hull to close up without the burden of my weight, it would therefore be difficult to spot. So from my small backpack of valuables I fished out my glasses, only needed for reading small type, finding splinters and the close examination of scraped and bashed fibreglass. By getting on my hands and knees in the shallow water, I could just about carry out a close examination of Mole's underside. Satisfied that the starboard side was without serious injury I turned Mole around and inspected the port side with the same results.

I couldn't believe we had survived this encounter unscathed and marvelled at the resilience of Mole's elderly fibreglass. I decided to celebrate with a mug of coffee and quickly set up the gas stove and kettle aboard Mole, before setting of again. Once back midstream I gave my guide a quick look and was somewhat annoyed to realise that I had failed to remember the warning of rapids. I was equally annoyed that I had failed to remember to look out for the remains of wharfs and quays, as Llandogo had been a busy Wye port and in addition, well known for building flat bottom barges until the end of the eighteenth century.

Just beyond Llandog, lay the village of Tellech, which interesting was the birthplace of renowned philosopher and mathematician Bertrand Russell, at Cleddon Hall in 1872; and the site of many ancient monuments. Local archaeological excavations have been ongoing for more than a decade, as Tellech was considered to have once been the most significant settlement in medieval Wales.

The weather was perfect and once again the land rose up on either side of the river, showing the Wye valley at it best. Following a few minor left and right turns, the river gained that distinctive rotting seaweed smell of estuaries and harbours at low tide. I'd obviously reached that part of the river subjected to the daily tidal ebb and flow. Next I was surprised to discover a catamaran sailing cruiser moored in the centre of the river. It didn't have the appearance of recent use, as there were plastic footballs, big lumps of polystyrene and all kinds of floating rubbish jammed between the twin hulls.

However, my biggest problem of the moment was my rear end. Even with my great pile of padding, it was increasingly painful to sit. My only option to gain any form of relief was to keep changing my sitting position, from one buttock to the other. I actually tried kneeling for a while, but this required facing towards the bow and rowing backwards so to speak, and wasn't successful. When suddenly, I had a brainwave. If I couldn't resolve the root cause of my discomfort, then I'd address the symptoms and from my first-aid kit sourced a couple of serious painkillers, which were washed down with some lukewarm pop. My analgesia kicked in pretty quickly and allowed me without the distraction of pain, to soak up the sheer magnificence of the Wye valley, bathed in warming sunlight.

CHAPTER 12

Romantic Tourism & Not!

Noon scorch'd the fields; the boat lay to;
The dripping oars had nought to do,
Where round us rose a scene that might
Enchant an ideot--glorious sight!
Robert Bloomfield

According to the map, my next stop at Brockweir Bridge could not be too far away, where I would be facing the unresolved problem of getting all my kit and caboodle to the campsite at the Tintern Old Station, almost a mile further on and a good way from the river. Although canoeists regularly camped at the Old Station site, managing to drag their canoes up the adjacent riverbank and transporting their equipment across the fields etc., it wasn't a suitable landing for either Mole or me. In spite of this, the weather and scenery were far too enjoyable, so I dismissed any forthcoming logistical concerns from my thoughts.

I was fascinated that such great poets as Wordsworth, Coleridge, Bloomfield and the like should be unanimous in their adoration of the lower section of the Wye valley. Officially designated an Area of Outstanding Natural Beauty, various sources claim that here was the birthplace of British tourism. Apparently in the mid-eighteenth century, Reverend Dr. John Edgerton, the then-incumbent at Ross, commissioned the building of a pleasure craft, specifically for talking parties of friends on regular river trips down to Chepstow. Thomas Gray, he of 'Elegy' fame, wrote of his river journey from Ross to Chepstow in 1771 *"Its banks are a succession of nameless beauties"*. Gray's further writings, along with the 1782 publication of Gilpin's *Observations on the River Wye*, served as the first illustrated tourist guide and helped turn the trickle of tourists into a flow.

Apparently by the nineteenth century, Wye valley tourism had turned from flow to flood. Not only had all the popular poets of the time visited the Wye and scanned a verse or two in its praise, but the rampaging Napoleon had put an end to the British taking the 'Grand Tour' of Europe, so the well-heeled and their retinues headed for the Wye valley. A number of accounts claim that *"thousands flocked to Ross in the summer months"* and I have to wonder if there was sufficient boats, beds and food, or did the sheer volume of people swamp the Wye and perhaps spoil its 'picturesque'?

I remembered the tale of London poet and theatre critic Clement Scott, who in 1883 set off for Norfolk in search of peace and tranquillity, away from the hustle and bustle of London. He decided upon using the newly opened Norwich to Cromer railway. Being unable to find suitable lodgings in Cromer, Scott set off along the coast. Eventually he came across a quaint mill and was offered accommodation. Such was the hospitality at the mill and surrounding landscape, that Scott was convinced he'd found his perfect 'rural idyll'.

So taken was Scott with his 'heaven on earth' with its swaths of poppies, that he named it 'Poppyland'. He became a frequent visitor to the mill and recounted his experiences in regular and descriptive letters to the Daily Telegraph. Needless to say, the thousands of people reading Scott's accounts also wanted to experience the *"innocent charm and tranquillity"* and flocked to 'Poppyland'. Of course, on discovering his beloved 'Poppyland' overrun with visitors, Scott was horrified and rued the day he'd shared his secret find. On a positive note, he did go on to marry the miller's daughter.

I was returned to the present by discovering Brockweir Bridge, which provides road access to the village of Brockweir and beyond from the A466 Chepstow road, was just ahead. My plan was that I had no plan at all, apart from eventually camping overnight which I hoped would be at the Tintern 'Old Station'. My guide recommended "landing at restored stone landing" just before the bridge on the left bank, which I presumed to be the historic 'Brockweir Quay'. What I did find was a unprepossessing stone structure, some forty-odd feet in length, which was covered in deep dried mud, left behind by some previous flood tide.

I nosed Mole towards what I mistakenly thought to be a few steps at the beginning of the quay, but found it difficult to hold station as the flow was quite strong. Fortunately, there was a narrow square section steel post with two mooring rings, driven into the bedrock. Grabbing Mole's painter I made a lunge for the post with one hand, while quickly tying a bowline through a ring with the other. At least I was moored and could now sit back and concentrate upon resolving the problem of getting all my stuff onto the landing, which was some eight feet above the water level.

I had to act fast as the tide was running out rather quickly, making the quay higher by the minute. Although appealing, I dismissed the idea of sleeping for twelve hours until the next high tide, when I could probably just place my boxes on the quay from a sitting position. There seemed to be another set of steps positioned central to the quay and a narrow slipway at the other end, possibly for getting small craft on and off the river. Needless to say, both these facets were designed to be used at high tide and so were of no use to me.

My only option was to use the now exposed large boulders at the end of the quay, which would allow me to get a few feet higher and then be able to place my boxes and bags on top of the landing. With Mole eventually emptied of cargo, I fathomed a mooring arrangement so he could be safely secured, but cope with the changing river height. Satisfied I'd done all I could to ensure Mole's security, I clambered labouredly up a narrow gap between the end of the stone quay and the riverbank. Once I'd arranged all my goods in a safe pile away from the water's edge, I sat down and contemplated my next move of getting to the Old Station.

After a brief period of time and without any flash of inspiration, I took a stroll and studied my surroundings. The area was magnificent, as was the village of Brockweir. Once again it was hard to believe that this idyllic spot had such an industrious history. Brockweir being the last tidal quay for boats travelling up the Wye from Bristol, saw much transferring of cargos between sea going vessels and 'Wye Trows', flat-bottom barges specially designed to travel the Wye. Originally the Trows were hauled up and downriver by teams of men, but following the construction of a towpath along the riverbank, men were replaced by horses.

Brockweir became the busiest port on the Wye and in addition to handling all the up and downriver cargoes, shipped vast amounts of iron and timber from the Forrest of Dean to Bristol. Brockweir also became a major centre for ship building, refitting operations and supporting industries. Apparently, between the sixteenth and seventeenth centuries, this genteel hamlet became notorious for 'lawlessness and rowdiness' due to the many stevedores, sailors and bargees. Perhaps Brockweir's sixteen public houses had something to do with it? Sadly the coming of the railways would make river transportation of goods all but obsolete by the mid-nineteenth century.

Adjacent to the quay, a garden wall bore an interesting plaque, with an excellent engraving depicting 'Wye Trows' being hauled by men and a photograph of the "La Belle Marie", a thirty-one-ton wooden-hulled steamboat, tied up at Brockweir Quay sometime before 1914. The vessel was used as a 'market boat' and must have sunk at her moorings, as the remains were discovered by the quay in 1967. One of her twin screws was recovered and is displayed just a few yards away.

While still pondering my predicament of getting to the Old Station, a car passed over the bridge and turned onto the quay. Out got a rather agitated lady who asked if I was waiting for the canoeists. Answering in the negative, I went on to explain that I had myself arrived by boat, indicating Mole, my pile of belongings and that I hadn't so far, seen any canoes. Not satisfied with my answers, the lady continued her interrogation about these missing canoeists and how I must have seen them. I gathered that somewhere upriver must be a group of youngsters of which one must be the progeny of this woman and I was somehow being held responsible for the group's non-appearance.

I suggested that as no other parents had arrived, the flotilla may not yet be overdue. The rather strange lady returned to her car, and after a few minutes lowered her window and continued her questioning from the comfort of her car. She would not accept that I had not seen, not passed, not been passed by or encountered by any means this group of canoeists. I often wonder how I manage to attract such people. I then had the flash of inspiration I'd been waiting for.

I stopped the incessant woman mid-sentence and began to explain my predicament. I went on at length about my health issues, my rehabilitation journey down the Wye and how I was about a mile short of my campsite at the Old Station and how I couldn't possibly carry all my boxes and bags. Finally I cut to the chase and suggested that while she was waiting for her daughter to arrive, she could perhaps transport me and my pile of stuff the short distance to my camp and be back in ten minutes or so.

Needless to say, she didn't offer to help, but quickly closed her window and reversed the car to the other end of the Quay, putting a good distance between us. On the positive side, I was now spared the endless nonsensical drivel. Approximately fifteen minutes later, four cars almost in procession passed over the bridge and turned onto the quay, shortly followed by a mini-bus with trailer.

The occupants left their vehicles and chatted happily together without the slightest hint of concern. As if on cue, a flock of yellow and red canoes arrived with weary-looking occupants. In quick time the combined efforts of parents and instructors had the youngster off the river and canoes strapped to the trailer. As quickly as they arrived they all departed, even the crazy lady. So once more I was on my own, with not a soul in sight, but it was a lovely spot to sit and do nothing.

Next over the bridge came a flock of pupils from some high school somewhere. It became obvious that the patch of grass beyond the quay was a teen meeting place, where a strange array of activities took place, from playing football to lighting fires. I had another flash of inspiration and from the less intimidating faction of mixed teens, I enquired whether anyone had the phone number of a local taxi firm.

A rather bored-looking female member of the group produced a very expensive-looking mobile phone and after scrolling through an extensive list of contacts, read out the number of a Chepstow taxi company. Unfortunately the girl could read faster than I could lock the numbers into my brain, but she obligingly agreed to wait until I had found pen and paper.

Using my own mobile I tried the number, which was answered in due course. I explained what I wanted, but the taxi man said he would be unable to get to me until six o'clock due to a previous arrangement and also there would be a surcharge of twenty pounds for me being out of his area. I agreed to wait the hour or so and to the surcharge, so to pass the time, helped myself to sizable snack, a drink, and listened to the news programme on my radio.

Five minutes past the hour of six o'clock, my taxi rattled over the bridge and drew alongside me and my pile of stuff. The rather bemused and seriously overweight driver got out, gave my belongings the once over, before indicating to which area of his vehicle I should stow my kit. Once loaded up, I gave Mole a quick check and then we set off. During our less than ten minute journey to the Old Station, my driver showed genuine interest in my predicament.

We turned left off the A466 Chepstow road into the access road for the Old Station. After some sixty yards we came upon a gap in the greenery on the left-hand side with a large wooden field gate, bearing a sign stating 'Camping Field'. I suggested to the driver that he should park up while I find someone in authority to inform of my arrival. My hurried amble found the railway coaches designated for officialdom to be closed, but I did find a lady still at work in the onetime 'Waiting Room' now converted to a café. The kind lady said I could camp anywhere in the field as there were no other campers and that she would wait until I was sorted to show me the toilet key 'arrangement'.

So it was just a matter of getting my stuff over the locked gate, selecting a bit of grass and pitching my tent. I think my taxi driver now felt sorry for me, as he insisted that I should climb over the gate and he would pass everything over to me. This did make the operation easier, so when we'd finished I paid and thanked the taxi-man. With polished expertise I soon had my tent up, cargo squared away and while taking in my new surroundings, sauntered back to the lady in the 'Waiting Room'.

The kind lady handed me the key to the toilets, to which was attached a large piece of wood. She went on to explain that if I returned to the campsite via the path up a steep incline behind the 'Waiting Rooms' rather than using the access road, I would see that the entrance to my field was via a wooden gate, which had a wooden box attached. So the golden rule was, when finished with the toilet key, it now had to be returned to the box on the gate. This was fine, but I wished I had known this before I pitched my tent. As my tent was at the other end of the field, my journeys to the loo had now doubled in distance, but it was only going to be for one or possibly two nights. I thanked the kind lady for staying behind and bade her goodnight.

I gave the Old Station one last look. From the 'Waiting Rooms'/Station Master's Office, to the signal box and train of three coaches, everything was extremely well maintained. Strangely I had feelings of melancholia. Although it was obvious that considerable effort had been made to preserve this railway monument, it was sad to see this once busy station without lines, passengers and of course, magnificent steam engines.

Before tackling the ascent up to the camping field, I made use of my toilet key. The facilities were exceptionally clean though probably Victorian. Amusingly, they were just how I remembered station toilets from my earliest train travels in the 1950s, lots of black stone, white tiles and very cold. With due diligence, I ensured I'd turned off the light and secured the door.

Having laboured my way up the steep path to my field, I passed through the gate and deposited the loo key in its box. I soon had my much needed meal underway and considered my lot. My campsite or field was a small meadow surrounded by mature trees and bushes of a good height. In the interests of wildlife conservation, the outer edges of the meadow had been left unmown, allowing a stunning display of multi-coloured wild flowers to prosper, which in turn played host to numerous coloured butterflies and insects. Surrounded by nature at its best and the warm evening sun, is when my adventure fulfilled my expectations.

I was feeling rather sleepy after my rather large helping of marvellous chilli and rice, when my mind turned to Mole. He was at risk, being vulnerable to both high tide and marauding vandals. I realised that I would never relax without confirming he was OK. So after putting all my cooking equipment inside the tent, I grabbed my valuables rucksack and headed for the path down to the Old Station.

From the station buildings I strolled along the old track way towards Brockweir Bridge. The rails had been gone for decades and in their place lay a carpet of moss, grass and wild flowers, with overgrown trees creating a kind of linear glade. This was a wonderful place and I wondered how many people had enjoyed a stroll here on a pleasant summer's evening. This direct route along the old rail track had me at Brockweir Bridge in no time, as it was far shorter than either road or river routes.

I clambered up the access way onto the bridge and was totally taken aback by my first sight of the river. The muddy river hurrying for the sea I had left earlier, was now a bizarre and surreal spectacle. The Wye had changed direction and was now being squirted back upstream, rapidly carrying with it a staggering amount of flotsam, jetsam and general rubbish. Every conceivable item of buoyant material, from large lumps of polystyrene, furniture, packing cases, pallets, plastic bottles, footballs, marker floats, to trees, bushes and lengths of sawn timber charged towards Monmouth. Trees and bushes with their root systems still attached stood erect, giving the Wye the appearance of a nightmarish conveyor belt to hell.

Mole's mooring system appeared to have worked well and he was at least meeting the barrage of rubbish bow-on. The bridge was an ideal place to witness this staggering degree of pollution. I thought it sad that all this rubbish could not be netted or captured before it was swept out to sea again, by the next receding tide.

I walked down off the bridge and onto the quay. On approaching Mole I noticed a black mark on his bow, just below where the hull meets the foredeck. Being curious, I moved closer and discovered the mark to be a perfectly square hole through the fibreglass. It soon became apparent that the size of the hole was precisely that of the two-inch steel cap on top of the steel post I'd tied Mole to. It would seem that the surging incoming tide had slammed Mole into the steel mooring post, which had in turn punched a hole through the hull. So my mooring system hadn't been perfect after all. Obviously a hole in the hull wasn't good, but as Mole's last voyage to Chepstow would be unladen, I was relatively satisfied that the hole would remain a good height above the water line and not let water in between the hull skins.

Three youngish chaps were also on the quay. One tried a fishing line amongst the strange lumpy Wye soup, while the other two looked on. Seeing me give Mole the once over, the trio enquired as to what I was about. They were interested in my trip and had themselves canoed the Wye around these parts many times. Seeing that I now had local knowledge at my disposal, it would be a good opportunity to enquire about the best time to leave the quay with regard to the tide and of course the good old mud at Chepstow.

I explained my apprehension over the last seven miles to Chepstow as my guide stated that it should only be attempted by "canoeists with reasonable experience". The trio were unanimous that I shouldn't have any problems providing that I closely follow the tide rather than going before it. One of the group recounted an experience where he for excitement purposes, rode the tide at speed to Chepstow. Such was the force of the river, that he was unable to make a landing on the pontoon by the Boat Inn and was swept on, managing to make landfall just before the Wye met the River Severn.

Another said that they had all mistimed the outgoing tide at one time or another and had been left high and dry some distance from the Boat Inn, but he foolishly had tried to cross the mud and warned in such circumstances to stay in the boat. My group concurred with my guide, in that I should have left Tintern *"not later than one hour after high water"*, which would mean leaving Brockweir, being two miles back upstream, around twenty minutes earlier. The next question addressed high water.

None of my new friends were confident about the precise time of tomorrow's high water. My guide stated *"High water at Tintern is four hours earlier than Dover"*. So when is high water at Dover? Although I had accessed the official website for Dover tides, I'd forgotten to make a note in my guide. A quick call home had my wife looking up Dover high water times on the internet. Following numerous calculations it was agreed by all, that by departing Brockweir quay at 9.15am the following morning, should ensure my safe arrival at the Chepstow pontoon.

Buoyed by the confidence extolled by my new friends, I felt I may actually survive Chepstow. I thanked the trio for their help and wished them well before setting off towards the campsite. Even though problematic, I was pleased to have designated Brockweir and the Old Station as my last overnight stop. I wished I'd thought about using a taxi for transporting my stuff to the campsite at my initial planning stage, it would have made things a little easier. Also, I kept forgetting 'Plan B', that if I'd been unable to find transportation, I could have just rowed Mole back upriver to a less public spot and slept aboard.

I gave the neatly mown grass, flower-filled planters and newly painted buildings of the Old Station one last look, before wishing all the ghosts goodnight and setting about the climb up to my field. This really was a wonderful spot. Whether I would hold a different view if the place was heaving with visitors, I couldn't say, but it was certainly an ideal place to visit and picnic. The lack of showering facilities would perhaps deter one from camping for more than a day or two, but for my needs it was perfect.

Back at my tent the light was beginning to fade and I was pretty well done in. I decided to finish off another perfect day with a mug of drinking chocolate, so unfolded my chair, sat and surveyed my kingdom. Again I considered how fortunate I was to have this experience. As the dark arrived, the calls of the night animals and birds began. So I readied for bed and was soon in the land of nod.

Away, away, from men and towns,
To the wild wood and the downs
Percy Bysshe Shelley

I was dragged from the depths of unconsciousness by some commotion going on somewhere around my tent. Something or someone was rustling or running against the bottom of my tent's outer flysheet, just a few inches from my head and then snagging the guy ropes. I was used to having various wildlife or campsite dogs trying to enter the tent in pursuit of food, but found by repeated slapping of the tent material near to the offender, generally frightened off whatever was lurking outside.

On one camping trip, a cow refused to be intimidated by my tent slapping, ploughed through all the guy ropes and demolished the tent in the middle of the night. On another occasion, my boys and I were awoken by a strange and loud crunching noise in the early hours. Eventually we discovered the culprit to be a tiny harvest mouse munching its way through our box of cornflakes. It was hard to believe that one tiny mouse could make such noise.

I gave the tent side a good slap or two and tried to go off to sleep again. Before I had fully returned to the land of nod, my nocturnal visitor returned, with much snuffling and disturbance of the flysheet on the other side of the tent. I was desperately tired and in no mood for playing games with some creature of the night, so gave the tent side another good slap. But this time, as I slapped the tent side my hand came up against something that I felt move through the nylon material.

I was now seriously annoyed. I refused to be subjected to the torture of sleep deprivation by some stray hound or perhaps Mr Fox who had come a calling.

I was out of my sleeping bag and had my head torch on in quick time. For some unjustifiable reason I checked my watch, it was exactly 2.15am which did nothing for my mood. I filled a pan with cold water to throw over the damnable mongrel, as I knew the shock of cold water would deter a dog from doing many things. I unzipped my tent door and stuck my head out. Much to my absolute amazement I discovered five or six youngish badgers engaged in brawling and general mayhem at the back end of my tent. Almost instantly, probably due to my head torch, the cete of badgers waddled off into the woods behind and were gone.

How amazing! How lucky was I? How many people get the opportunity to be so close to such magnificent creatures. I had to stop myself from phoning somebody and telling of my experience. I felt guilty for thinking evil thoughts about young Mr Brock and siblings for disturbing my sleep. Back in my sleeping bag I considered my good fortune and how once again the animals of the Wye valley had played a prominent role in enhancing my adventure. Before drifting off to sleep I mused that it wouldn't be a big surprise to anyone that I had seen badgers in a field close to a place called Brockweir!

The annoying ringtone of my mobile phone's alarm brought me out of a most fitful sleep at 7.30am. I had one hour and forty-five minutes to get myself sorted and leave Brockweir Quay in order to catch the tide at the right time for my final voyage to Chepstow. With my porridge underway, I completed my ablutions with water from my plastic container, rather than the hiking down to the Old Station. With breakfast consumed and flask filled, I piled my pots and pans haphazardly into the tent to be dealt with later, donned my windjammer, cap, life jacket, rucksack and made off towards the Old Station.

My first port of call was at the train of railway carriages to pay my camp fees, but found them to still be closed. Next call was to the café, where I found my nice lady from the previous evening and staff beavering away. I purchased a large ham salad baguette, a piece of chocolate cake and a can of soft drink for my lunch aboard Mole. Following a brief question and answer session upon my exploits so far, I thanked my inquisitors and said goodbye. The weather was again very good. Given it was still relatively early in the day, the sun was quite warm, but cold enough in the shade of the tree canopy over the old rail track to warrant the continued wearing of my windjammer and life jacket.

It was a pleasant experience strolling back to Brockweir Quay, I felt like a boatman of centuries past about to do a day's toil aboard a river craft. Starting the day with a pleasant amble was far more enjoyable than taking down the tent, packing up and lugging my great pile of stuff down to the river. I wondered whether Mole would benefit from being without the weight of his cargo, or would he be less stable?

Crossing over Brockweir Bridge I was heartened to see Mole was still where I'd left him the night before. There was still loads of rubbish in the river, but worryingly, it was almost stationary and wasn't racing to the Bristol Channel. So had I misjudged my start time and was I in fact, too late for the outgoing tide? Realising the water level was almost to the top of the quay, it was obvious that it was near or just after the 'slack-water' period, usually an hour after high tide and before the tide starts to recede. So perhaps I was worrying unduly; according to my watch I was only four minutes behind schedule. It had to be now or never. I decided that if I felt at risk from being shot out into the River Severn like a cork, then I would drive Mole ashore anywhere and address the implications later.

One advantage of the high water was that it enabled me to step directly into Mole from the quay. After fitting the oars, I untied the moorings, manoeuvred Mole into midstream and set off. Not being fully confident about my situation with the tide, I didn't know whether I should go as fast as possible or as slow as possible, but in the final analysis decided to accept my fate and go as normal.

I was soon away from the quay and out from under Brockweir Bridge; the speed of the river seemed to be actually less than normal.

I gave up trying to avoid the floating debris and just ploughed through it, albeit that the odd baulk of timber gave Mole's hull a hefty thump. Once again I was treated to a cloudless sky and everywhere I looked was magnificent. As the river started a long turn to the right, we passed but couldn't see, the Old Station or my tent. I caught up with a small group hiking along the riverside path, that I had encountered previously. Apparently they had all breakfasted well a few miles back at St. Briavels.

Approaching the consecutive villages of Tintern Parva and Tintern, the river began a slow turn left and with it came a definite and significant increase in flow. Here the main Chepstow road ran next to the river as it arced round. A few houses, inns and hotels stand on the roadside, squeezed in-between the steep hillside towering above. The habitation was almost quaint if not almost picturesque, but certainly worthy of a photograph or two. Attention to navigation was required here, as a number of craft were moored mid-stream and were swinging around on their bow lines.

After Tintern appeared another bridge, with the right-hand buttress adorned with scaffolding. Before the bridge the Wye became wider and 'choppy', which as Mole was lighter and higher in the water, made for a strange undulating ride. By the high water mark along the riverbank, I approximated the river had already dropped four feet or so. I wasn't sure if this was a good or a bad thing.

I was soon rewarded with a view of the spectacular ruined Tintern Abbey above the tops of the riverside trees. Founded by Cistercian monks in 1131, the Abbey continued until dissolution by Henry VIII in 1536. The abbey lay empty and was apparently subject to persistent pilfering of roof lead, timber and stonework, which brought about its eventual ruin. I was amused to learn that the abbey was *"cleaned up"* around 1760, as it had become a 'tourist hotspot' of the Wye Valley. To experience the full splendour of the abbey and gaze upon its vaulted aisles, it should be accessed from the A446 Chepstow road.

The pain in my posterior reminded me I'd forgotten to attach the seat padding, so shipped the oars and opened the fore-deck compartment. Much to my horror I discovered the padding to be missing and realised that I had left it behind at the tent. I briefly considered tying Mole to some tree and hiking back to the campsite, as I firmly believed that I could not complete my journey without some form of seat padding. The time delay would, however, make landing at Chepstow on the current tide impossible.

Eventually, my brain engaged and I realised that it was now warm enough to dispense with my windjammer, which I folded into a tight pad and lashed to the seat with some spare cord. My life jacket would have been extremely comfortable to sit upon, as its soft buoyancy sections had facilitated many a good afternoon nap. I discarded this idea, as to drown so close the end of my journey would be very annoying.

Close to the left bank, the wooded escarpment of the valley achieved a respectable height. I thought but wasn't too sure, that I'd spotted the 'Devil's Pulpit', a pillar of limestone amongst the hilltop trees, renowned for providing spectacular views over the Wye valley. From my research on the subject, I discovered this lump of stone gained its notoriety from legend, which claims *"the pulpit was used by the devil to cajole the monks toiling below at the abbey, in order to persuade them to join him!"*

Our course took several long curves in either direction, followed by a tight right turn. I found this tidal, muddy river, sinister and definitely intimidating. On the left, limestone cliffs soared from the riverbank. After studying the cliffs for a while, I eventually spotted a couple of climbers at work, belaying their way to the top. The current was still dragging Mole along, so I shipped the oars and drifted around the loop, while watching the climbers and finishing off the last of my cider. With my brief rest over, I picked up the oars again.

The Wye continued with long turns left and right. Knowing exactly where I was proved a little difficult, as views of the adjacent countryside were obscured by the riverside bushes and trees. The muddy riverbanks still wet from the outgoing tide, dazzled in the bright mid-day sun. I was rather done in, so declared it lunch time. After finding a recumbent and comfortable position which was difficult without my all kit, I let Mole drift in his preferred manner of backwards while I set about my baguette.

With lunch break over, I returned to the oars. The tide was still pulling Mole along, so I didn't have to exert much effort to maintain a decent pace. I hoped I could keep going without my usual afternoon siesta, so to provide a little distraction from the toil and strain, I listened to the last chapters of *Three Men in a Boat* on my MP4 player. From the 'wet line' on the riverbank, I estimated the fall in river level to have now increased to around ten feet.

After a tight right-hand loop, the river ran straight for a good distance before starting another turn to the left. Although the water was relatively flat and Mole rode along quite smoothly, the pain in my rear end had become intolerable, so in the absence of suitable seat padding, I reverted to my heavy-duty analgesics. As we started round a left-hand bend, I caught my first glimpse of Chepstow Castle. Eventually the whole of the castle and its buildings came into view on the right-hand bank, standing tall upon limestone cliffs.

Apparently William the Conqueror, realising the strategic importance of Chepstow, instigated the building of the castle shortly after his arrival in 1067. Like every old structure along the Wye, Chepstow Castle received a good pounding during the English Civil War. Originally, held by the Royalists, it fell to the Parliamentary forces in 1648. Needless to say, the castle became a major point of interest to those eighteenth-century Wye tourists.

Rowing directly below the castle, I could appreciate how compelling and intimidating it would have seemed to some would-be invader. I was so fascinated by the castle, that it was a surprise to arrive at my most important landmark, the lattice steelwork bridge which carries Bridge Street. This bridge signified that my final destination, the pontoon by the Boat Inn, was just around the bend.

Once out from under the Bridge Street bridge, I hugged the right-hand bank. The water level seemed to have dropped considerably without me noticing. I now started to panic, believing that I was too late to make the landing. Eventually the pontoon came into view and it was no longer floating; the water was just up to the front side. My only option was to row towards the pontoon as fast as possible and try reach it before the river disappeared. Then someone pulled the plug out of the bath!

I was amazed how quickly the water was vanishing. I drove Mole's bow up the drying bank as far as possible, then stuck an oar deep into the mud at Mole's stern to stop him being dragged out any further by the receding tide. Then there I was, left high and dry. I was fifteen feet of deep mud away from my landing and the successful conclusion of my journey. I had missed the opportunity of mooring onto the pontoon and walking ashore by a few minutes. Oddly, it didn't bother me at all.

I tested the depth of mud all around Mole with an oar and it was certainly impassable on foot. If my life had really depended upon it, I could have crossed the mud by lying flat and using the oar shafts to distribute my weight. However, I would be totally exhausted and covered in some pretty evil-smelling mud.

I was quite content to sleep, rest or listen to my radio until the tide returned. I did have one major problem though, that when the tide did return, I could be washed back to Brockweir. I needed to tie Mole to the pontoon somehow, before I could relax. Along the top edge of the pontoon some six feet above the mud, were three sets of large cleats for tying craft to. There was one set at either end and one set in the middle. These double cleats were like 'cow horns' and around ten inches high, the middle set were possibly within lassoing range.

I tied my two longest ropes together and formed a sliding loop at one end. I had five or six goes at throwing the loop over the cleat, but got nowhere near. I tried standing on Mole's foredeck to get me nearer to the pontoon. After endless attempts at lassoing the cleat I was shattered and needed to rest. I poured a cup of coffee from my flask, sat down and considered my options again.

I could hear people somewhere behind the stone retaining wall at the Boat Inn, I just need one of them to look over so I could attract their attention. I was sure some kind person would come down onto the pontoon, catch my rope and secure it to a cleat. My problem was that Mole was obscured behind the pontoon, so unless I stood up, no one would know I was there. I started a routine of standing and watching the wall for possible help, followed by ten attempts with my rope, then sat and rested. I was rather disgusted with myself for not managing the simple task of lassoing something only fifteen feet or so away.

Then some thirty yards away, the head and shoulders of some chap appeared as he leant upon the wall, but faced away from the river and me. I could see his head which was adorned with a cycling helmet and shoulders attired in a coloured cycling jersey. He was obviously chatting intently to someone and periodically lifted a pint glass to his mouth. I tried politely hailing this chap, whistling and performing inoffensive waving gestures, but to no avail as the chap was too focussed upon whoever he was speaking to. I tried the plastic whistle tied to my life jacket, but it was no louder than my own 'fingers in mouth' method.

I suddenly remembered my 'Acme Thunderer' whistle which was fastened to my Swiss Army penknife. Not only were these two items valued components of my emergency kit, but veterans of many an adventure. Without doubt, with all these walls and cliffs to reverberate the sound, my Thunderer would certainly awaken the dead of Chepstow and more importantly, attracted the attention of the preoccupied cyclist. As quickly as my hope were raised, they were dashed again, as I discovered my highly effective whistle and emergency kit had been left behind at the Tintern Old Station campsite.

The object of my cyclist's attention turned out to be a young lady, who now also leant against the wall, which was good, as the cyclist was looking more in my direction. I repeatedly whistled, shouted and waved my arms like someone demented, but to no effect. I have enjoyed cycling as both man and boy, but had by now developed utter contempt for this chap attired in cycling garb and wished upon him a curse of a thousand punctures!

With my first throw of my next repetition, I 'bull's-eyed' my quarry. Unbelievably, the loop at the end of my rope rounded the cleat and stayed put. I gingerly pulled the rope to slip the knot tight, then gave it one hard pull. My rope was finally and soundly secured to the pontoon, the other end I tied back onto Mole. At last, I was safe from the perils of the raging incoming tide. When the tide did return, using the rope I could pull myself towards the pontoon and tie Mole near enough for me to climb out.

As I started to relax, I could feel the onset of fatigue and need to sleep. Mole was lying almost diagonally up the dried out riverbank, which made for an uncomfortable sleeping position. Using the oar I'd driven into the mud to stop Mole being dragged further down the bank by the outgoing tide, I levered the bow down the bank a couple of feet or so, until he was at right angles to the slope of the riverbank and able to provide me with a level sleeping position.

I could soon feel myself drifting off to my favourite place of nod, but not before the realisation of my achievement. I had done it! Albeit that I was stuck in the mud, I had made it to Chepstow and so far, I was still alive!

CHAPTER 13

Mud, Mud, Glorious Mud!

*"I have never been lost, but will
admit to being confused for several days."*
Daniel Boone

Following a fitful sleep, there's something marvellous about opening your eyes, to a cloudless blue sky. Sitting up, I took in my surroundings for the first time. I'd been so preoccupied with securing Mole that I'd noticed little of my new environs. My beautiful Wye, now some forty feet away and below, was a shallow, placid ribbon of muddy water, draining wearily onwards to the River Severn. The four craft moored mid-channel, presently faced upstream with the outgoing tide; their change in direction would be useful in alerting me to the return of the tide.

I knew the Wye had one of the greatest tidal ranges, but trying to estimate the actual fall in water level by the still-wet mark on the riverbank was difficult, without there being something of known height to compare it with. By my best guess, I reckoned the water level had dropped by at least twenty feet.

My mud was beige in colour for a few inches down, then grey and after that, it became black, horrible smelly stuff, which had the load-bearing qualities of rice pudding. Even though the tide had long gone, the surface of the mud was maintained in a liquefied state, by constant running water.

The opposite riverbank was a tree-covered limestone cliff that rose straight up some fifty feet from the river bed and continued on downstream past the new-looking bridge carrying the A48. I could see little behind me, as my view was obscured by the pontoon, several dried out boats and the stone retaining wall. The only movement I could see anywhere apart from the odd crow and gull, was the traffic passing over the A48 bridge. My folded life jacket was an excellent cushion and at least made sitting almost tolerable.

To help pass the time, I brought my journal up to date while listening to the early evening news on my radio. I retraced the day's journey on my map and was amused to discover that I was a temporary guest of Monmouthshire, Wales, as the border with Gloucestershire, England was only forty feet away in the middle of the river.

Whether it was due to my forced inactivity or not I didn't know, but I was starting to feel seriously hungry. It was the first time in eleven days that I'd been separated from my mountain of provisions and was beginning to panic. I did still have my can of soft drink from the Old Station, but was saving it to celebrate my arrival on dry land.

I was just contemplating eating a handful of mud, when I remembered the box of emergency rations my elder son James had given me, stowed in Mole's foredeck compartment. After much struggling I eventually pulled the ration's cardboard box through the access hatch and set about the exploring the delights within. I selected a foil pouch of chicken curry and rice that could be eaten either hot or cold, an energy bar and handful of boiled sweets. Fortunately the box contained a set of plastic eating utensils so I wouldn't have to eat the chicken curry with my fingers. Along with a comprehensive range of survival foods and condiments, the kit had soups and all the usual beverages requiring hot water and interestingly, sachets of electrolyte solution, water purification tablets, soap and toothpaste. So if the Wye ever did return again, I could drink it, wash in it and even clean my teeth with it.

I felt decidedly better for sustenance, which was washed down with my reserved celebrative can of warm pop. Although the sun was much lower, it was still warm and most enjoyable, so adopted a reclined position to feel the sun on my face and relieve the pressure upon my rear end. Sometime later, the movement of a large bird caught my eye, as it flew along the cliff face to a sizeable niche in the rock opposite my position, which after hesitating momentarily, it disappeared into.

Almost immediately the bird reappeared and with consummate ease soared upwards and disappeared away over the cliff top. I was treated to a number of repeat performances by this raptor, which I believed to be and had confirmed the following day, a magnificent peregrine falcon. Given the amount of back and forth trips this bird was making, there must have been a sizeable brood of chicks up in the cliff face. Apparently, patrons of the Boat Inn behind me had been observing the pair of peregrines for some time.

Being so engrossed in observing this majestic bird, I'd failed to notice the four craft below me were no longer gently pulling on their moorings and were in fact, in the process of changing their direction. So at last the tide had turned. It also occurred to me that I didn't have to wait until the Wye reached full high tide for me to reach dry land, as all I needed was enough water to float Mole up to the pontoon. The rate at which the incoming tide rose up the sides of the river was impressive. The four nearby craft had now turned and were straining at their moorings in the opposite direction. Upstream, a few boats previously dried out, now with water under their keels, swayed around on their painters.

I suddenly realised that the surging tide would drag Mole to the end of his painter and I may not have the strength to pull him the twenty feet back towards the pontoon. I would then have to sit and wait until the tidal power subsided. To be on the safe side, I decided to tie a 'Lorry driver's knot' on Mole's painter. This knot works like a 'block and tackle', multiplying the pulling effort by three times, and is generally used for tying loads onto trucks etc. This would help me overcome the force of the incoming tide and enable me to pull Mole to the pontoon sooner rather than later.

I needed to tie my knot as far as possible along Mole's painter for the maximum effect. So after placing an oar on the mud a few feet away to support my weight, I carefully placed one foot on it while retaining the other on Mole's seat. With some additional stretching, I managed to tie the knot a good way along the rope. Needless to say, it took several attempts before I remembered how to tie the ingenious knot system correctly.

I'd barely retrieved my oar and sat down before the returning Wye lapped against and then surrounded Mole's hull. As soon as I felt Mole being moved by the flow I increased the tension upon his painter and continued to do so as his buoyancy progressively increased. By the time Mole had clear draft under his keel, I'd managed to pull him considerably nearer the pontoon with the assistance of my clever knot and after a few more pulls on the rope, I was alongside and able to tie on.

So there I was, finally moored next to the Ship Inn pontoon. After stowing the oars, I put my rucksack and life jacket on top of the pontoon, then sorted out Mole's bow and stern mooring. After giving everything one last check I climbed up and onto the pontoon. Rather stiffly I ambled over the first and second pontoons and connecting walkway. I'd forgotten that the Ship Inn landing consisted of two small pontoons joined by a short railed gangway, which I'd been unable to see from my position in Mole.

Once at the retaining wall I ascended the flight of stone steps and upon reaching the top, was somewhat taken aback to see around thirty patrons of the inn sat at the numerous tables, engrossed in conversation and merriment. It was odd to think that I'd been sat for hours, stranded in isolation while this lot had only been a few yards away.

I had almost expected the crowd to rise to their feet and give rousing cheer and applause, in recognition of my worthy accomplishment. For had I not successfully navigated one hundred and four miles of the mighty River Wye and survived? Not one person looked in my direction or even acknowledged my presence. I remember reading of polar explorers who upon reaching the North Pole, experienced the anticlimax of there being no actual pole, monument or reception committee.

Passing through the happy throng of revellers I made for the entrance to the inn and then to the bar. At least I would as planned, acknowledge and celebrate my safe arrival at journey's end with a glass of local brew. My thoughts turned to the problem of retrieving Mole from the river so I asked the barman about the key to the gates in the retaining wall, stating that I was led to believe that the Ship Inn was the custodian of said key. The barman went off to make enquires but returned none the wiser, but suggested I should ask the local boat people.

I never really viewed the gates as a viable option due the number of boats that would have to be moved in order to make way and equally, from my pre-journey inspection of the gates, it would seem that they hadn't been used for years and would be troublesome to open, even if I had found the key. However, I decided not to burden my thoughts with Mole's repatriation until tomorrow, better to use the day or what was left of it to wallow in self-satisfaction of achieving and experiencing a wonderful adventure.

I left the inn and after satisfying myself that Mole was coping with the buffeting incoming tide, headed for where Mole's trailer was chained up. The trailer was still as I had left it so it was next to my car, which also seemed to be in one piece. I open the door and got in. Never in my entire life time has a seat, chair, sofa etc. felt so good. The relief to my rear end was such, that I just sat with my eyes shut, exuding great long sighs of relief. Although I could have quite happily just sat for hours enjoying the luxuriant comfort provided by my car seat, I somewhat reluctantly drove off and headed back to my tent at Tintern Old Station.

Due to a minor navigational error, I took an unplanned but pleasant tour of Chepstow and while stopped at the traffic lights controlling the one-way system through the sixteenth-century town gate, I realised that I was still producing long sighs of relief. My car had been subjected to direct sunlight all day, so I had all the windows and sun-roof open to dispel the heat, which in turn now allowed the most amazing smell from some nearby fish and chip shop to enter in.

Such was the marvellous smell, that I immediately became ravenous and began serious cravings. As the traffic lights turned green and we moved through the old arched gateway, the establishment purveying the fare of my desire shortly appeared on the right. After some sharp manoeuvring and avoidance of double yellow lines, I was in and out with a bulging polystyrene box of wonderful golden deep-fried potato delicacies. It had been ages since I last tasted the most British of gastronomic delights and these beauties didn't disappoint.

Once back at the campsite, I gathered up all the used pans and bowls etc. from previous meals and headed down to the station, to take advantage of the hot water. Leaving the now washed pans and plates to drain, I took a brief stroll around the station before availing myself of a wooden bench bathed in the warm evening sun. It was a little odd to have the entire station area and campsite to myself. It was as if I'd been made custodian, being responsible for the establishment during my short stay, almost like being marooned on the proverbial desert isle.

Although the old place had a definite air of stillness and tranquillity, visions of all the hustle and bustle of arriving and departing steam engines and passengers coming and going, easily formed in my mind's eye. For the second time I'd experienced such vivid images, so quickly collected my now dry pots and headed back to the tent, before I actually saw the 20.15 train from Monmouth arrive.

Back at the tent I got the kettle going, so I could watch the sun going down over the Wye valley with a good cup of tea. Close to the back of the tent, I noticed the recent and comprehensive work of moles, the four-legged ones. This, I thought, would probably account for the close proximity of the badgers the previous evening, as the moles' earthworks would probably expose a good source of earthworms. While pondering the moles and badgers scenario my thoughts turned to the other Mole. As he was only fifteen minutes away by car, I decided that if I gave him one last check before nightfall, I would be far happier.

Back at the Boat Inn, I scaled the steps up the retaining wall and strode down the gangway of the now fully floating pontoon. I found to my annoyance, that Mole had been moved and rather than the double moorings I had left him with, he was now tied by a single rope to some other craft tied onto the pontoon. It would appear that some chap arrived in a rib (rigid inflatable boat) and wanted to moor on the end of the pontoon and found Mole's presence to be an inconvenience to his own objectives, so tied him onto another small boat around the side of the pontoon. He or she had moored their rib bow and stern, but not Mole.

Mole may have survived until next morning and could have swung around with the changing tides without coming to any harm. However, it wasn't the 'belt and braces' approach which enabled me to sleep soundly. After pushing and pulling at other boats, I managed to make a space for Mole along the side of the pontoon and re-established his double mooring. Being satisfied that I had done everything possible to assure Mole's safety, I returned to my car. I admit to briefly considering casting off the offending rib and letting it be taken ten miles upriver or out into the Bristol Channel and beyond, then the owner would really experience inconvenience.

By the time I was back at the campsite I was shattered and with nightfall immanent, I was soon in my sleeping bag. I reflected upon the day. Yet again the Wye had fulfilled all my expectations for new experiences and adventures. So much had happened since my stroll down the old railway line to Brockweir Bridge first thing this morning. I was still reflecting upon the day when I succumbed to sleep.

Initially I was brought to consciousness by some unknown factor. Lying there in the dark, I eventually realised that my awakening was not due to some nocturnal animal activity, but undue pressure upon my bladder. Given the emergency of the matter, I quickly stuck on my sandals, grabbed my coat and headed across the field to collect the key to the station's washroom. Whilst fighting intense bladder pressure and being halfway down the sloping track to the station, it occurred to me that I could have just availed myself of a nearby bush or piece of grass. After all, I would only do what every other animal wandering about at this time would do and equally, there was nobody around to be offended.

With milliseconds to spare I overcame the washroom's Victorian door lock and reached the convenience. By my watch it was exactly one o'clock. I did wonder if wandering around the station at this time in the morning was wise, given that I might meet some long-passed ticket collector or station master. Ablutions completed, I turned off the lights and relocked the door. I waited for a short while in the doorway to allow my eyes grow accustomed to the pitch-black. Eventually I could make out the line of trees rising up along the track back to my field, so turned left out of the doorway and walked slap bang into some unworldly ghoul!

There are no words to describe the heart-stopping terror I endured in that moment. Equally, I cannot claim to have responded fearlessly to my strange encounter. However, when one expects to have the entire Old Station and surrounding grounds to one's self, it was quite a fright to walk into an elderly Canadian lady wearing a large padded coat and hood at one o'clock in the morning. As the lady scared me, I scared the lady, so simultaneously we vented such startled cries, as to bring the lady's companions, thinking that some misdeed had befallen their friend.

Eventually, I had the washroom door open and lights on. My early morning visitors began to explain why they had virtually scared me to death. Although I did find it amusing to be surrounded by highly animated octogenarians from Canada, dressed like Yukon trappers. My new overseas friends were apparently two brothers and wives from Vancouver, fulfilling their dreams by touring the UK in a 1960s hippy-type Volkswagen campervan. They'd hired the van in Bristol, crossed the Bristol Channel Bridge into Wales and then driven around in circles for hours.

Having found themselves back at the end of the Channel Bridge and being very late, they searched their tourist guides for the nearest campsite, which turned out to be the Old Station. They arrived to find the whole place in darkness, apart from the light shining from the washroom windows. One of the ladies volunteered to investigate and was approaching the washroom when the lights went out. She had apparently, tentatively found her way around the back of the building, when she was almost bowled over by some wild screaming banshee.

My new Canadian friends were all very tired and in desperate need of the washroom facilities, so being custodian of the station, I agreed to let them complete their bedtime requirements before securing the building again. I pointed out to their consternation that the station didn't allow caravans or campervans, but assured them that given their circumstance, I didn't think anyone would mind them parking up for the night. They did seem to cheer up considerably when I told them that the station café did a wonderful breakfast.

This little group were stereotypes of everyone's favourite grannies and grandpas. I had considered telling them where the key to the washroom was kept during the night, but wasn't happy at the thought of them climbing the steep track up to the box on the field gate in the darkness. So I made an executive decision and decided to leave the washroom unlocked all night, for which they were very grateful.

Unsurprisingly, the next morning I slept late but awoke quiet refreshed. With breakfast consumed I collected up my wash kit and mused over the previous night's antics as I ambled down to the station washroom. Given the hour I wasn't surprised to note that my new Canadian friends had already departed. Next I sauntered up to the line of stationary railway carriages and finally found a person to whom I could pay my camping fees and return the washroom key.

Now it was just a question of retrieving Mole. My tent I decided could be left in situ, as I was now preoccupied with Mole, and would collect it upon my homeward journey. Once back at Chepstow I parked up by the Ship Inn and climbed the steps over the river's retaining wall to check that mole was still where I'd left him. Seeing my faithful old friend gently tugging at his moorings was very emotional and I found it necessary to cross the pontoons and express my appreciation for all his good works.

Whilst studying all the issues and obstacles that would have to be surmounted to repatriate Mole to his trailer, I spotted the my new friend Mac working on his boat some fifty yards away upon the esplanade. Mac had volunteered to keep an eye on my car and trailer during my absence and also, help with getting Mole from the river and over the retaining wall, should I actually make it back alive, he had joked. According to Mac, dragging small boats up the riverbank and over the wall was a common occurrence and there was always a source of willing helpers among the boating fraternity, should we require additional assistance.

We walked along the wall inspecting the riverbank in order to find a possible spot suitable to haul Mole. Fortunately, some thirty yards from the pontoon, the angle of the riverbank changed from near vertical to a more gentle slope, with a good carpeting of tufted grass which would make it easier to slide Mole up the bank. With our extraction plan formulated, Mac untied Mole and negotiated his way from the pontoon to the riverbank by stepping from boat to boat, while guiding Mole around the assorted craft. Eventually, Mac was near enough to my position to throw me the painter, enabling me to pull Mole to our selected patch of riverbank.

Mac joined me by the water's edge and between us we pulled Mole up the grassy bank and up onto the top of the retaining wall. While we had Mole balanced in this situation we changed our position to the esplanade side of the wall and I recorded Mole's predicament with a photograph. We slid Mole off the wall and down onto the esplanade. With Mac's expert assistance the whole process of getting Mole back onto dry land had been relatively straight forward and easy, for which I was extremely grateful.

I soon had the trailer's wheel back on, which I had removed

twelve days previously to stop it being pinched, and with Mac's help lifted Mole onto the trailer. Once Mole was securely roped to the trailer, I asked Mac to take a snap of me and Mole at the end of our adventure. I wanted to show my appreciation of my good friend Mac's help with a drink at the now open Ship Inn, which he declined but was finally persuaded to partake in a celebrative cup of coffee. We chatted about my Wye adventure and about boats in general and with coffee drunk, we left and I thanked Mac again and said goodbye.

Once Mole and trailer were united with my car I went back and had one last look at the river where my journey had ended, then set off back to my camp at the Old Station. It all felt very odd. This was the first time in thirteen days not to be on the river. I really missed those mixed feelings of adventurous excitement and trepidation when loading up Mole each morning and setting off downriver, wondering what new experiences and perils the Wye had in store.

I was soon back at the Tintern Old Station and parked up as near as possible to the camping field main entrance gate. I had no appetite for the conscientious packing away of camping kit, so everything was uprooted and dumped in the back of the car as was. It was another warm day with lots of blue sky. I spent a few minutes leaning on the gate, just taking in the landscape. The camping field or meadow without my tent was in itself picturesque. The wild flowers of the unmown surrounding section, slightly animated by the gentle breeze were magnificent.

Before leaving I drove down to the station buildings and had one last look around. I was glad to have camped at the Old Station and with hindsight; it was well worth the transportation difficulties. It had contributed considerably to the great adventure, even though I had been scared half to death by badgers and octogenarian Canadians. I was still sure I had sensed the presence of many long-gone station personnel and was almost disappointed that they hadn't made an appearance. Having assured myself that Mole was well and truly secured to the trailer and the trailer was well and truly secured to the car, I departed.

I avoided the direct route home and instead, chose to follow the Wye as closely as possible until Hereford. At times the road would run alongside the river providing a clear view, or I would only catch a glimpse every now and again through a gap in the riverside trees.

Initially, I was overcome with melancholy with the ending of my adventure, but conversely heartened when realising how fortunate I had been, to even have the opportunity to undertake such a journey and perhaps more importantly, that my physical condition had allowed me to do so.

The Wye had been amazing. Memories of all the humorous incidents and encounters, far too numerous to relate in this minor tome, will stay with me forever, as will those of all the helpful, generous and fascinating people I met along the way. I feel it's only fitting that my spirit guide, the Reverend William Gilpin, should have the last word in describing the River Wye and all its glory.

"Having thus analyzed the Wye, and considered separately its constituent parts: the steepness of it bank, its mazy course, the grounds, woods and rocks, which are its native ornaments; and the buildings, which still further adorn its natural beauties; we shall now take a view of some of those pleasing scenes which result from the combination of all these picturesque materials."

William Gilpin

River Wye Adventure Recipes

Mole's Spam & Noodles (for one)
1. Chop into small squares, one small can of Spam (or any pork luncheon meat).
2. Finely chop half a red pepper and half an onion.
3. Cook one portion of medium egg noodles, drain and keep covered.
4. Stir-fry meat and vegetables in rapeseed oil until cooked.
5. Add the noodles to the meat and vegetables and stir-fry until noodles are heated through.
6. Stir in soy sauce to taste and remove from heat.

Mole's Chorizo Couscous (for one)
1. Finely slice approximately 150mm of chorizo (or any dried spiced sausage)
2. Chop one red pepper, half an onion and quarter one tomato.
3. Prepare as instructed, one 125g packet of Moroccan-style couscous and cover.
4. Stir-fry chorizo, pepper and onion in oil until cooked.
5. Remove from heat and stir in one table spoon of hoisin sauce.
6. Return chorizo and vegetables to low heat, stir in couscous until heated through.
7. Remove from heat and add quartered tomato.

Mole's Corned Beef Sweet Chilli Pasta (for one)

1. Place one 110g packet of quick pasta and sauce into pan.
2. Make up one sachet of chicken and vegetable cup soup as per instructions.
3. Pour soup mix onto pasta and stir.
4. Bring soup and pasta mix to the boil and simmer until pasta is almost cooked, then remove from heat and cover.
5. Chop half an onion and one small tin of corned beef; fry until onion has browned.
6. Add the pasta and soup mix and stir well.
7. Add black pepper and sweet chilli sauce to taste; continue to stir until pasta is fully cooked, then remove from heat.

Mole's Riverside Banana & Custard (for one)

1. Place half a 75g packet of instant custard powder into a bowl.
2. Boil three quarters of a mug (2.5cls) of water (must be boiling), pour onto instant custard powder and mix until thickened.
3. Slice one banana and stir into custard.

Mole's Flapjack recipe:

Ingredients:

200g butter.
80g soft brown sugar.
5 tablespoons clear honey.
3 tablespoons golden syrup.
400g porridge oats.
110g mixed dried fruit.
2 tablespoons sliced almonds.
2 tablespoons smooth peanut butter.

Preparation:

1. Butter a 13" x 9" baking tray.
2. Put the oats, mixed dried fruit and sliced almonds into a mixing bowl and mix well.
3. Place the brown sugar, honey, butter and peanut butter into a large saucepan and heat gently while stirring continuously.
4. Once the butter, honey and peanut butter has combined, stir well and remove from heat.
5. Pour the butter mixture over the oats, fruit and nuts. Ensure that the ingredients are mixed well.
6. Pour the mixture into the prepared tray and spread evenly, making sure the surface is flat.
7. Bake for 25 minutes in a preheated fan oven at 160 degrees or until golden brown, but do not overcook.
8. Remove from oven while the mixture is still slightly soft.
9. Cut the soft mixture into suitably sized oblong shapes and allow to cool and harden.

Lunch at Wyecliffe Weir, Herefordshire

Lunch at Kerne Bridge, Herefordshire

Hereford Cows, Symonds Yat, Herefordshire

Monnow Bridge, Monmouth

Stunning Bigsweir Bridge, Gloucestershire

Glorious Rive Wye, Gloucestershire

Old Station Campsite, Tintern

High and Dry, Chepstow

Reference Sources

Wye Canoe? Canoeist guide to the River Wye

Environmental Agency Wales

Welsh Canoeing Association

Ordinance Survey Maps

WyeNot.com

Welsh Tourist Board

Powis Tourist Information Centres

Hay-on-Wye Tourist Information Bureau

National Library of Wales, Courtfield Estate Records

BritishListedBuildings.co.uk

The Historic England Archive

www.brantacan.co.uk/wyebridges

Hereford Tourist Information & Travel Guide

Hereford Council

Forest of Dean Local History Society

National Trust

Site of Special Scientific Interest, Great Britain.

Natural England

Open Buildings

Forrest of Dean & Wye Valley

www.inspirational-quotes.info

The National Archives

Wikipedia

Burgum Family History Society

Gloucestershire Archives

The Chepstow Society

Wye Valley AONB

Bishopswood House

Observations on the River Wye – William Gilpin

Tintern Abbey & Romantic Tourism in Wales – Scholarly Publishing Office, University of Michigan.

Literary Norfolk

Quotes

Preface:
1. Kenneth Grahame – *Wind in the Willows*

Preamble Ramble:
1. Kenneth Grahame - *Wind in the Willows*

Introduction:
1. Spike Milligan – Headstone Epitaph
2. Marcus Aurelius – *Meditations*

Chapter 1:
1. Chay Blyth – *At One with the Sea – Alone Around the World* by Naomi James
2. Tom Fort – *Downstream*
3. Frederick Sanger – Nobel Banquet speech 1980

Chapter 2:
1. Roald Amundsen – *The South Pole*
2. Leonard Nimoy – @TheRealNimroy

Chapter 3:
1. Lao-tzu - *Tao Te Ching*
2. Jawaharlal Nehru – *The Discovery of India*

Chapter 4:

1. Amelia Earhart – Official website
2. Ferris Bueller – Character from 'Ferris Bueller's Day Off'
3. William Gilpin – *Observations on the River Wye*

Chapter 5:

1. Joe Brown – *The Hard Years*
2. Peter Bonthron – *My Holiday on Inland Waterways*

Chapter 6:

1. Anon – The Franklin Square Song Collection
2. Lewis Carroll – 'A Boat Beneath A Sunny Sky'

Chapter 7:

1. Aldous Huxley – *Texts & Pretexts*
2. W. H. Davis – *Leisure*

Chapter 8:

1. Mike Gafka – 'Inspirational Coaching'
2. Dr. Loretta Scott – Quotes from 'Aid & Assistance'

Chapter 9:

1. Anon – Unattributed
2. Omar Khayyam – *The Rubaiyat*
3. Robert Bloomfield – *The Banks of Wye*

Chapter 10:

1. Percy Bysshe Shelly – title unknown from 'Prometheus Unbound'

Chapter 11:
1. Roberto Assagioli – *Psychosynthesis*
2. P Bonthron – *My Holidays on Inland Waterways*

Chapter 12:
1. Robert Bloomfield – *The Banks of Wye*
2. Percy Shelley – 'The Invitation'

Chapter 13:
1. Daniel Boone – *Adventures*
2. William Gilpin – *Observations on the River Wye*

About the Author

Although not 100% recovered from his 'Post Viral Fatigue Syndrome', by maintaining his 'diet, exercise and rest' regime, the author went on to undertake the following challenges and adventures:

Cycle 1,052 miles unsupported from Lands End to John O'Groats;

Walk Wainwright's 200 mile Coast to Coast Route;

Summit the 3 national peaks of Ben Nevis, Snowdon and Scafell;

Compete in the London Triathlon sprint event with his 2 sons;

Cycle/camp the 232 mile Hadrian's Cycleway;

Complete the 24 mile Yorkshire Three Peak Challenge in 13 hours;

Cycle/camp 600 miles from the French Atlantic coast to the Mediterranean;

Cycle/camp the 1,100 mile River Rhine from the Swiss Alps to the Hook of Holland;

Cycle up Mont Ventoux, the iconic 'Tour de France' climb.

*

To see the photographic journal of the author's river adventure, along with further information upon the River Wye, visit:
www.theriverwye.co.uk

Printed in Great Britain
by Amazon